THICH NHAT HANH

MODERN SPIRITUAL MASTERS
Robert Ellsberg, Series Editor

This series introduces the writing and vision of some of the great spiritual masters of the twentieth century. Along with selections from their writings, each volume includes a comprehensive introduction, presenting the author's life and writings in context and drawing attention to points of special relevance to contemporary spirituality.

Some of these authors found a wide audience in their lifetimes. In other cases recognition has come long after their deaths. Some are rooted in long-established traditions of spirituality. Others charted new, untested paths. In each case, however, the authors in this series have engaged in a spiritual journey shaped by the influences and concerns of our age. Such concerns include the challenges of modern science, religious pluralism, secularism, and the quest for social justice.

At the dawn of a new millennium this series commends these modern spiritual masters, along with the saints and witnesses of previous centuries, as guides and companions to a new generation of seekers.

Already published:
Dietrich Bonhoeffer (edited by Robert Coles)
Simone Weil (edited by Eric O. Springsted)
Henri Nouwen (edited by Robert A. Jonas)
Pierre Teilhard de Chardin (edited by Ursula King)
Anthony de Mello (edited by William Dych, S.J.)
Charles de Foucauld (edited by Robert Ellsberg)
Oscar Romero (by Marie Dennis, Rennie Golden,
    and Scott Wright)
Eberhard Arnold (edited by Johann Christoph Arnold)
Thomas Merton (edited by Christine M. Bochen)

Forthcoming volumes include:
Flannery O'Connor
Edith Stein
G. K. Chesterton

THICH NHAT HANH

Essential Writings

Edited by
ROBERT ELLSBERG

Introduction by
SISTER ANNABEL LAITY

ORBIS BOOKS

Maryknoll, New York 10545

Eleventh Printing, June 2010

Copyright © 2001 by Thich Nhat Hanh

Published by Orbis Books, Maryknoll, NY 10545-0308

All rights reserved.

Grateful acknowledgment is made to Parallax Press for permission to reprint material by Thich Nhat Hanh. For information about the books excerpted here, other works by Thich Nhat Hanh, and other publications on Engaged Buddhism, contact Parallax Press, P.O. Box 7355, Berkeley, California 94707.

Excerpts from *Living Buddha, Living Christ* by Thich Nhat Hanh, copyright © 1995 by Thich Nhat Hanh. Used by permission of Riverhead Books, a division of Penguin Putnam, Inc.

Excerpts from *Going Home* by Thich Nhat Hanh, copyright © 1999 by Thich Nhat Hanh. Used by permission of Riverhead Books, a division of Penguin Putnam, Inc.

Cover photograph © Karen Hagen Liste

No part of this publication may be reproduced or transmitted in any form or by any means, electronic or mechanical, including photocopying, recording, or any information storage or retrieval system, without prior permission in writing from the publisher.

Queries regarding rights and permissions should be addressed to:
Orbis Books, P.O. Box 308, Maryknoll, NY 10545-0308.

Manufactured in the United States of America

Library of Congress Cataloging-in-Publication Data

Nhât Hanh, Thich.
    Thich Nhat Hanh : essential writings / edited by Robert Ellsberg.
        p.   cm. – (Modern spiritual masters series)
    ISBN 1-57075-370-9 (pbk.)
    1. Religious life – Buddhism. 2. Buddhism – Doctrines.   I. Ellsberg, Robert, 1955-   II. Title.   III. Series.

BQ5410 .N464 2001
294.3'4 – dc21

                                                        00-054342

Contents

Sources

Being Peace (Berkeley, Calif.: Parallax Press, 1987).

Call Me by My True Names: The Collected Poems of Thich Nhat Hanh (Berkeley, Calif.: Parallax Press, 1999).

Cultivating the Mind of Love: The Practice of Looking Deeply in the Mahayana Buddhist Tradition (Berkeley, Calif.: Parallax Press, 1996).

The Diamond That Cuts through Illusion: Commentaries on the Prajnaparamita Diamond Sutra (Berkeley, Calif.: Parallax Press, 1992).

For a Future To Be Possible: Commentaries on the Five Mindfulness Trainings, rev. ed. (Berkeley, Calif.: Parallax Press, 1998).

Fragrant Palm Leaves: Journals 1962–1966 (Berkeley, Calif.: Parallax Press, 1998).

Going Home: Jesus and Buddha as Brothers (New York: Riverhead Books, 1999).

The Heart of the Buddha's Teaching (Berkeley, Calif.: Parallax Press, 1998).

The Heart of Understanding: Commentaries on the Prajnaparamita Heart Sutra (Berkeley, Calif.: Parallax Press, 1988).

Interbeing: Fourteen Guidelines for Engaged Buddhism, 3d ed. (Berkeley, Calif.: Parallax Press, 1998).

Living Buddha, Living Christ (New York: Riverhead Books, 1995).

The Long Road Turns to Joy: A Guide to Walking Meditation (Berkeley, Calif.: Parallax Press, 1996).

Love in Action: Writings on Nonviolent Social Change (Berkeley, Calif.: Parallax Press, 1993).

Our Appointment with Life: Discourse on Living Happily in the Present Moment (Berkeley, Calif.: Parallax Press, 1990).

The Path of Emancipation (Berkeley, Calif.: Parallax Press, 2000).

Present Moment Wonderful Moment: Mindfulness Verses for Daily Living (Berkeley, Calif.: Parallax Press, 1990).

The Raft Is Not the Shore: Conversations toward a Buddhist-Christian Awareness, by Thich Nhat Hanh and Daniel Berrigan (Boston: Beacon Press, 1975; Maryknoll, N.Y.: Orbis Books, 2001).

Stepping into Freedom: An Introduction to Buddhist Monastic Training (Berkeley, Calif.: Parallax Press, 1997).

The Sun My Heart: From Mindfulness to Insight Contemplation (Berkeley, Calif.: Parallax Press, 1988).

Teachings on Love (Berkeley, Calif.: Parallax Press, 1998).

Touching Peace: Practicing the Art of Mindful Living (Berkeley, Calif.: Parallax Press, 1992).

Transformation and Healing: The Sutra on the Four Establishments of Mindfulness (Berkeley, Calif.: Parallax Press, 1990).

If You Want Peace, You Can Have Peace

Sister Annabel Laity

The venerable Thich Nhat Hanh is a Buddhist monk of the Vietnamese meditation school. "Thich" is the title given to all Buddhist monks and nuns in the Vietnamese tradition. It is a transliteration of the clan name Sakya and means that a monk belongs to the family of Shakyamuni Buddha. Nhat Hanh is a name he was given at the time of ordination. It means "One Action." To his friends and students, however, he is more affectionately known as "Thây," which means Teacher. That is how we shall refer to him here.

The number of those who look to Thây as their teacher extends far beyond those he has personally instructed. Through his many books, translated into twenty-two languages, his teachings have become known around the world. It has been said that Thây and the Dalai Lama are the two best-known Buddhist monks and teachers in the world today. We are fortunate to have on our planet people who are compassionate enough and brave enough to embrace the world with arms of caring action. Like the Buddha they are just human beings, and yet they help us see how any one of us human beings has the capacity to achieve such compassion. Thây is such an example of someone who has truly helped the world. His teaching is not just in the form of talks and books but in the way he lives his daily life. It is not limited to one particular group of people who are called Buddhist or even to people who consider themselves adherents of a spiritual path. One could say that the core of Thây's teaching is simply mindfulness. Such mindfulness, although it is the heart of the Buddha's teachings, can be practiced by anyone of any religious faith or none at all.

Thây has lived through the suffering of war and violent conflict in his own country, and yet he never finds any suffering so small that it is unworthy of compassion. He is a truly happy person who knows how to love and forgive everyone. For those who wish to understand him, however, it is valuable to understand the events and circumstances that formed him. Thây has said that he is who he is because of what he has lived through.

Thây was born with the name Nguyen Xuan Bao in 1926 in the province of Quang Tri in Central Vietnam. Vietnam, at that time, was under French colonial rule. When a country is occupied in this way, it is in danger of losing its very nature and soul. To prevent this many Vietnamese in the early twentieth century promoted a revival of Buddhism as a means of strengthening one of the most beautiful and wholesome factors of Vietnamese culture. Thây's early life was spent in this atmosphere of Buddhist renewal.

In a later poem entitled "Looking for Each Other," Thây would write, "I have been looking for you, Bhagavan (the Lord Buddha), since I was a tiny child." The poem goes on to conclude that when we do find the Buddha, we realize that we do not have to look anywhere outside ourselves. Every time we discover the Buddha outside of ourselves, it is only a reflection of the Buddha within. Thây's own first memory of discovering the Bhagavan goes back to when he was nine years old. He was looking at a picture of the Buddha seated in meditation on the cover of a Buddhist magazine. The beauty and peacefulness of this image deeply moved him, and it has remained with him ever since. This experience was an important factor in his decision to devote his life to monasticism.

Thây also remembers how, at the age of twelve, he was inspired by the ideal of the hermit who retires from the world in order to devote himself to a life of spiritual practice. At this time he went on a school outing to a mountain where a hermit was known to live. He left the party in order to seek out this hermit only to find his cave empty. But then he heard nearby a wonderful sound like the most beautiful piano music. It was coming from a spring of fresh water. Thirsty from his climb, he was able to drink from this cool source. It was much more than a source of water. It was the source of life and the source of understanding and happiness. In that source he found the true holy man. Though at the time he was perhaps not able fully to conceptualize this insight, he remembers remarking to himself, "I have drunk at the source of life." Such an experience, though it goes far beyond conceptualization, has the power to change forever the direction of one's life. Afterward Thây shared with his school friends his intention to become a monk, and he was joined by five other boys in this resolution.

Thây was only sixteen when he entered the monastery called Tu Hieu, a few miles from the center of Hue on a hill amid pine forests. This monastery had been established with royal approval toward the end of the nineteenth century. It had vegetable, flower, and fruit gardens and a couple of water buffaloes that supplied manure for the temple gardens (their milk was reserved solely for the baby buffaloes). When Thây first entered the monastery, he was responsible for looking after the buffaloes, taking them out to pasture every morning. As the buffaloes grazed, he would work on memorizing his assigned Chinese texts. As a novice Thây studied and practiced under the direction of a master, carefully observing the virtuous qualities of this experienced monk and learning how to manifest them in his own life. The novice formation in the Buddhist tradition is very simple. The novice learns to be present in whatever he or she is doing. While closing the door you learn to be truly present while closing the door. While cooking you are truly present in the cooking. While washing your hands you learn to be wholly present as you wash your hands. The practice is for the mind and the body to be present in one place and in one time. The novice learns short poems in order to see the significance of the most mundane actions of daily life. One recites these poems silently while doing any action in order to be aware of what one is doing. Thus, after meeting Thây in 1966, the Trappist monk Thomas Merton remarked that he could recognize that Thây was a real monk simply by watching him close the door.

Whenever Thây talks about his time as a novice, he radiates happiness. Without doubt those were some of the happiest days of his young life. Sometimes the young monks went hungry and sometimes they hid under the altar to take a short nap when they were sleepy. But despite the mental rigors and material deprivations, the harmonious community life brought about a deep peace and joy. Nevertheless, even in the monastery it was impossible to ignore the signs of strife and suffering in Vietnam. During World War II the French occupation gave way to invasion by the Japanese. When, after the war, Vietnamese nationalists declared independence, the French, with U.S. support, initiated a war to reimpose their colonial rule. The war caused widespread death and destruction. As the fighting approached, even Thây's own monastery, Tu Hieu, was evacuated for a time.

Soon after his full ordination as a Buddhist monk in 1949, Thây moved to Saigon to lend his efforts to an emerging movement for the reform of Buddhism. A younger generation of Buddhist monks was eager for Buddhism to emerge from its ivory tower and to become more engaged with social realities. Thây collaborated in the development of the South Vietnam School of Buddhist Studies, whose curriculum included modern languages as well as scientific and cultural studies.

In 1954 Vietnam was divided at the 17th parallel into two countries, communist in the north and capitalist in the south. The repressive regime of Ngo Dinh Diem in South Vietnam was supported by the United States government. Diem, who was a Catholic, regarded the Buddhist leadership as a threat to his government and instituted a series of discriminatory and repressive measures. At the same time, a new era of war was beginning between the government of South Vietnam and the communist government of North Vietnam and its supporters in the South. Though Thây was never interested in becoming involved in politics, he saw the necessity of all Buddhist groups unifying in order to be able to provide a real alternative in society. His wish was that his country be governed in accord with the principles of compassion and non-discrimination which are found in the teachings of the Buddha. But he believed this was not just the responsibility of the government. The role of any church, whether Buddhist or Christian, should be to help people organize themselves, their families, and their society to live in accordance with these principles.

In 1955 Thây was asked to become the editor of a journal called *Vietnamese Buddhism*. This was a wonderful opportunity to encourage unification of all the different schools of Buddhism in Vietnam. To Thây and other young Buddhists the journal was an anchor in an otherwise confused and anxious time. But two years later the journal was closed, ostensibly for financial reasons. Thây believed the real reason was that his proposal for Buddhist unification was unacceptable to the leadership of the different congregations. The closure of the magazine seemed like a great failure, and for Thây it led to a period of deep inner questioning. Seeking a quiet space for healing and reflection, he and some friends purchased a piece of land in the mountainous forest of Dai Lao, about a hundred miles from Saigon. There they established their own contemplative community, which they called Fragrant Palm Hamlet.

The following years were relaxed and happy. The usual rigors of the monastic rule were replaced by a very simple way of life with a certain freedom of activity. Monastic life is generally organized with a strict schedule of practice activities and the assignment of work and studies by the monk or nun who oversees the community. The Fragrant Palm community was intimate enough and sufficiently experienced in the practice not to need this kind of organization. Anyone who had a project he wished to realize would simply announce it to the community and invite others interested in joining in. For instance, someone might say, "Today I wish to go into the forest to look for orchids," and whoever wanted to was free to go along.

Meanwhile, despite the joy and harmony of his community, Thây's writings were increasingly opposed both by Buddhist leaders and by the dictatorial Diem regime. When in 1962 Thây was offered a fellowship to study comparative religion at Princeton University, his friends encouraged him to accept. Thây was certainly needed in Vietnam, but there were too many obstacles from the government and the Buddhist clergy in the way of his vision for Buddhist renewal.

This time in the United States was difficult; it was his first protracted separation from his homeland. On the other hand it brought new opportunities for reflection and the strengthening of his spiritual practice. During this year he wrote a little book called *A Rose for Your Pocket*. In later years, Thây remarked that he had been teaching Buddhism for many years but it was not until he wrote this book that he truly came to a deep understanding of what he taught. Written for an Ullambana Celebration (the Buddhist equivalent of Mother's and Father's day), *A Rose* was a gift for all those who still enjoyed the happiness of having their mother alive. In writing Thây managed to touch in a poignant way his real grief at the loss of his own mother but also his ability to transform that grief by experiencing his mother's constant presence in his life. In reading the book today one is struck by themes that would appear in his later books. Like much of Thây's writing, it does not pretend to give a lesson in morality. It is more like an encouragement and an invitation to us to enjoy the most simple and beautiful things in life.

After one year at Princeton Thây was invited to teach at Columbia University. However, by 1963 the oppressive measures of the Diem regime in Vietnam had become intolerable. Buddhists were prohibited from displaying the Buddhist flag during the Buddha's nativity celebration. Electricity and water supplies to the most important Buddhist temples in Saigon were cut off. In the face of this situation and the atmosphere of mounting crisis, a prominent Buddhist monk, Master Quang Duc, publicly immolated himself as a silent protest.

Thây worked hard to make these events in Vietnam known and understood by the American public. With great sympathy and understanding he read the work of Dietrich Bonhoeffer who, during his own sojourn in the United States, had longed to return to Germany to suffer with his fellow citizens under the Nazi regime. Finally in November 1963 the harsh Diem dictatorship ended with Diem's assassination during a military coup. This did not lead to peace. But the repressive measures of the Diem era had accomplished a change of consciousness among the Buddhist leadership and created a new openness to reform. With much hope of contributing to this process, Thây cut short his stay in the U.S. and returned to Saigon. There, by the end of 1964, he was able to witness the fulfillment of a long dream: the founding of the Unified Buddhist Church of Vietnam.

Among Thây's most significant projects was the founding of the School of Youth for Social Services (SYSS), a pure example of what he would come to term "engaged Buddhism." The aim of the school was to repair the social damage of the intensifying war. Students were sent into the villages to serve the people in the four areas of health, organization, education, and economic development. Thây was personally involved in their training, not so much in the technical aspects, but in how to establish good relationships with the villagers. This was not easy. The villagers had been mistreated by the government and by the Americans, who only wanted to set up strategic villages for the purposes of fighting communism. Now, quite naturally, they no longer trusted anyone who wanted to come and tell them how to improve their village. Thây trained his young social workers how to live as a friend to the village people. In order to set up a village school the young social worker would play with the children and then take a few hours of the day sitting in the shade of a tree to teach them how to read and write. After a while, when it would rain one day and the lesson could not continue outside, someone would offer a room in their house for the class to take place. Then, when the class became too big to fit in that room, people would offer their own materials or labor in order to build a simple classroom. Thus the villagers never needed to feel anything was being imposed upon them. This is what Thây refers to by the French word *bricolage*. It means that we create something from the materials we already have at hand. We do not have to bring in anything from the outside. The villagers benefited from this work of love, and the students too were happy, because they saw that there was something they could do in this terrible situation of war to relieve the suffering. Soon there were many more applicants than the school could accommodate.

While spending his weekends in the villages, Thây spent the rest of the week teaching and writing at the Institute of Higher Buddhist Studies, which he had helped to found in Saigon. These two streams expressed Thây's realization that action and wisdom must go together. If we study it is not to store up knowledge but to deepen our understanding. Our understanding, in turn, can only deepen as we put it into action.

In other ways as well Thây sought to express this integration of understanding and action. He compiled a new set of fourteen "mindfulness trainings" to be the guiding light of a new religious order called (in English) "The Order of Interbeing."

Before leaving Vietnam in 1966 Thây ordained six of his young social workers in these trainings. It was not a monastic ordination. Thây has said that he was not attracted to the idea of ordaining disciples. The ordination was a celebration of the most wholesome things we can commit ourselves to in times of the greatest devastation and destruction.

Although the SYSS was taking measures to bring real relief, the war was becoming more dreadful all the time. One village was bombed three times and rebuilt three times. People were ready to give up hope. Every time the village was bombed Thây gave instructions for it to be rebuilt. What is the point of rebuilding a village when you know it will be bombed again? He told them that if they did not rebuild the village it would mean that they had given in to despair. During these years Thây continued to write in favor of reconciliation. Because of his refusal to take sides he was considered an enemy by both communists and the American-backed government in South Vietnam. Many of his students and colleagues were killed, and he too narrowly escaped an attempt on his own life.

The roots of the war were not just in Vietnam. In order to go to the source of the war Thây returned to the United States in 1966. The occasion was a seminar on Vietnamese Buddhism in March of that year, but this seminar was followed by a speaking tour arranged by the Fellowship of Reconciliation, an organization of religious pacifists. His aim was to inform the North American people about what the war was doing to the Vietnamese people and to make a desperate call for peace. It was in May of this year that Thây met with the famous American Trappist Thomas Merton. Thomas Merton immediately recognized a sense of deep religious brotherhood with Thây, and he went on to write an introduction to Thây's first English book, *Lotus in a Sea of Fire,* a Buddhist perspective on the war in Vietnam. Thây met with senators such as William Fulbright, who were opposed to the war, but also with Secretary of Defense Robert McNamara. Thây met twice with Martin

Luther King, Jr., who went on to nominate him for the Nobel
Peace Prize.

It was an exhausting time in the service of peace. Thây had
speaking engagements in every important city in the United
States. He would wake up in the middle of the night with no
idea where he was. Often he encountered hostile questioners
who accused him of communist sympathies. But more often au-
diences were touched by his obvious sincerity, and they were
moved by the opportunity to attach a human face to the distant
suffering of the Vietnamese people. As word of his activities
reached Vietnam, he was denounced by the South Vietnamese
government, which refused him permission to return. He was
now not simply an emissary of peace but an exile.

Thây has spoken about the homesickness he first felt on
knowing that he was not allowed to return to Vietnam. Now
he says that everywhere is his home. But in the first six months
of his exile Thây longed to see the species of birds and plants
to which he had been accustomed in Vietnam. He even had a
recurring dream in which he found himself unable to ascend a
hill that symbolized his native land. Eventually as he engaged
in the practice of dwelling in the present moment he was able
to be in touch with the flora and fauna, play with the children
of North America and Europe, and to see them all as equally
wonderful manifestations of life. From the point of view of the
deeper teachings of Buddhism everything that is over there can
be found over here. Nothing is lost and nothing is added on.
When we practice looking deeply at the moon over here, we
see that we are in contact with the moon over there. All the
various species of animals, plants, and minerals over here are as
beautiful and true as their brother and sister species in Vietnam.
Truly there is nothing to miss. Moreover, once we have experienced something deeply it is always there for us to touch again.
Thây talks about his experience of the fragrance of the grapefruit flower. In the American northeast there are no grapefruit
flowers, and yet Thây, sitting in a library in New York, could

experience deeply that fragrance. And so his recurring dream came to an end.

Nevertheless, while he adjusted to his new and unfamiliar setting, he continued to suffer the separation from his students and fellow-workers in Vietnam, knowing of their ongoing peril and suffering. In 1967, while Thây was in Paris, he heard that one of his first Order of Interbeing disciples had immolated herself in front of the Tu Nghiem pagoda in Saigon. Her name was Nhat Chi Mai (which means Single Branch of Plum Blossom). Later he received news of the death of Thây Thanh Van, head of the School of Youth for Social Services. He was killed by an American military truck. Thây Thanh Van was dearer to Thây than a blood brother. When Thây heard the news of his death, he closed himself in his room for more than two months.

In 1969 Thây was requested by the Unified Buddhist Church of Vietnam to set up the Buddhist Peace Delegation in Paris, the site of ongoing peace talks between North Vietnam and the United States. The Buddhists hoped there would be room in the discussions for a voice representing the common people of Vietnam and their great yearning for peace. Thây was assisted by one of his earliest co-workers in Vietnam, who had joined him in exile: Cao Ngoc Phuong (who later became Sister Chan Khong, or "True Emptiness"). In Paris they established a small international family of practice as a basis for the work which had to be done. From this base Thây made contact with religious and humanitarian leaders and groups in Europe and North America.

Eventually, in 1975, the war in Vietnam came to an end with the victory of the communist forces. But the new regime was no more hospitable to the practice and development of engaged Buddhism, and it became clear that Thây would not be welcome to return. The Unified Buddhist Church, to whose development he had given much time and energy, was outlawed. Its ministering monks were imprisoned. Only one Buddhist Church, sponsored by the government, was allowed to function. Thây remained in exile in France.

Some years before this, Thây had begun looking for a hermitage outside the city where he could write and grow vegetables and herbs. In a derelict farm in Fontvannes, a hundred miles south of Paris, a new refuge was found. In 1975 they were able to move in. Thây had been teaching the history of Vietnamese Buddhism at the École Pratique des Hautes Études in Paris, and now in the hermitage he could complete three volumes of a history of Vietnamese Buddhism. From the hermitage he could also continue to be in touch with what was happening in Vietnam: the imprisonment of monks who belonged to the Unified Buddhist Church and of writers and artists who did not follow communism. Thây's life was still in danger from those who did not understand his refusal to take sides in the conflict in Vietnam. A trap door was made in the ceiling of his room in case he should need to escape.

During these years Thây continued to travel in Asia and other parts of the world as part of the Buddhist Peace Delegation. When Thây was in Singapore in 1976 to attend the World Conference on Religion and Peace, a group of women refugees from Vietnam brought to his attention the plight of the refugees who were drowning on the high seas in the Gulf of Siam. Certain countries such as Singapore refused to accept refugees and pushed their unseaworthy boats out to sea again, where the people on board were destined to drown. Thây personally witnessed this scene and spoke very movingly about it to the delegates at the conference. They responded by inviting Thây to lead a rescue operation. The aim of this operation was to rescue the refugees in boats and to take them to Australia and the island of Guam. The operation rescued some eight hundred refugees from drowning. The difficulty was the failure of the U.S. and Australian governments to raise the quota — pitifully small — they would accept. Thây's aim was not simply to relieve immediate suffering but also to bring the suffering of the refugees to the attention of the North American and Australian people so that they would themselves force their governments to raise the quotas.

By 1982 the number of visitors and meditation students who wanted to come to Thây's hermitage in the Forêt D'Othe had grown too large to be accommodated. On two abandoned farms in the southwest of France Thây established a new community center, Plum Village, which remains his home to this day. As well as being a practice center, the community began as a foyer for refugees. Here refugees for whom Sister True Emptiness had been able to obtain visas could come and stay until they were ready to enter French society. Thây did not impose any strict regime of spiritual practice on the refugees who came to Plum Village. They were expected to grow crops on the land and to help organize the month-long summer retreats. His intention was that they could heal the wounds of war while living in this safe environment. Today the summer family retreats at Plum Village respond to the needs of a different kind of meditation student. While still catering to the needs of refugees, the greater number of participants are European and North American. It is a place where anyone can come in order to learn the art of living in the present moment with right attention and deep awareness.

Thây has never seen Plum Village as his center. He has allowed it to develop in its own way according to the needs of those who come there to practice. At first Thây did not see the necessity for monastic ordination in Europe and North America. The mindfulness trainings of the Order of Interbeing and the Five Mindfulness Trainings seemed to be ample guidelines for those who wanted to serve Plum Village as permanent residents. However, the publication of Thây's life of the Buddha inspired some people with a desire to pursue a monastic life in the spirit of the community of the Buddha. At their request Thây allowed them to receive monastic ordination. The monastic community of the Order of Interbeing in the West received its first members in 1988. Since then the community has continued to grow until it has reached more than one hundred members from fifteen different countries. These members live principally in Plum Village in France, but monastic houses have been established in Vermont and Southern California in the United States.

As he approaches the age of seventy-five, Thây remains as vigorous as ever, teaching wholeheartedly the fourfold Sangha of monks, nuns, laymen, and laywomen throughout the world. He travels extensively to give teachings and lead retreats. He is in touch with people from all professions and walks of life, always seeking to learn more so that his teachings can be relevant to healing the real ills of our world. If he meets politicians, he endeavors to persuade them to adopt social and economic policies which will reduce violence. He has led specialized retreats for veterans from the Vietnam War, for children and young people, psychotherapists, business people, artists, and environmentalists. He plans to lead retreats for biologists and physicists as well, increasingly convinced of the close relationship between recent scientific discoveries and the ancient teachings of Buddhism.

People ask Thây if he regrets not being able to return to Vietnam. He replies that he is in Vietnam now. His books and tapes, although officially banned, are widely circulated underground. Many monastics living in Vietnam teach the engaged Buddhism which they have learned from Plum Village. The monks and nuns whom he has nurtured in Plum Village are able to return to Vietnam, and every time they return Thây feels he returns with them. Nevertheless there is no doubt that it would be of great benefit to the Vietnamese people if Thây could return, even if only on tour. It would heal wounds in the hearts of many and encourage us to feel that the communist regime is not wholeheartedly opposed to those who are practicing a path of peace, joy, and understanding.

Some people, concerned that Thây will not be in this world as a spiritual figurehead forever, are fearful of the future. Thây has no such fears. He says that he will be climbing the green hill of the twenty-first century with all his disciples in the form of a Sangha. Sangha means community of practice. Thây has no intention of appointing a single successor. The community which has grown under his guidance will continue the practice and teaching that Thây received from the Buddha and that he has handed on in a unique way suited to the needs and the suffering of the present day. That community will also continue to find new Dharma doors specifically suited to transforming the suffering of our times. That community will not live as individuals but as a single body sharing experience and insight in order to use the non-individualistic eyes, the eyes of the Sangha.

Thây has never been accorded a special position by the Buddhist hierarchy or by any other organization. He lives a very simple life with his Sangha, either in Plum Village in France or on tour in different countries of the world where he travels. Thây enjoys every moment of his life, and organizes his day so that it can be enjoyable for himself and for others.

When I first met Thây he used to call me to come and help him with this or that. In fact it was Thây who helped me more than I helped him. One day Thây suggested that I come and help him print several hundred copies of the Plum Village newsletter. I arrived early in the morning ready to start work straightaway. I knew we had a busy day ahead. Thây's frame of mind was somewhat different from mine. He suggested that we have a cup of tea. Offering tea to his disciples is one of Thây's favorite ways of teaching. When Thây drinks tea, he only drinks tea. He does not think about the work that has to be done when the tea is finished. Thây is concentrated and relaxed while drinking tea and his disciple learns to be the same. After the tea Thây suggested a walk. I was a little surprised: with so much work to do, how could there be time for a walk? I followed Thây outside and we walked on beautiful little roads in the French countryside. After some time of walking, in which I managed to forget all about the matter of printing, we returned and went into the printing room.

It was a little chilly and we needed to light the wood stove in order for the printing process to work properly. Thây lit the stove with evident enjoyment and without any haste. We then had to make the printing plates. With a great deal of patience Thây taught me how to do this. First he introduced me to the printing machine. He said that it had the nature of a buffalo. We had to know its nature, what it could do as well as its shortcomings, and then we could work efficiently with it. This buffalo had three speeds: fast, medium, and slow. Thây said he had only ever used the slow speed. The fast would be far too noisy and if you used the medium and there was a mistake in the printing you would not have time to stop the machine before it had wasted quite a bit of paper. I was surprised at the end of the day when Thây told me that we had almost finished: there were only a couple of more pages to be printed the next morning.

Working with Thây like this is a very important lesson. You feel that you are living in eternity and there are no deadlines. In spite of this Thây accomplishes a great deal in terms of writing, teaching, gardening, and designing. Whatever he does he does with zeal and application so that it is more like an interesting play than toil. The name Nhat Hanh means One Action, and all Thây's actions are done in the same spirit of relaxation and enjoyment. To whatever action Thây applies himself, it becomes a way of making peace.

1

Present Moment
Wonderful Moment

"To dwell happily in the present moment," was a common phrase of the Buddha. Often he advised his disciples, "Do not lose yourselves in the past, do not run after the future. The past no longer is, the future has not yet come." Thây does his utmost to encourage his students to be in the present moment. Once, when organizing a retreat in Plum Village, we had some problems of an organizational nature which seemed to me to be of paramount importance at that time. I saw Thây in the garden and related the problem to him. Rather than tell me directly what I should do he led me to a small magnolia tree and asked whether I had enjoyed the fragrance of this flower yet. There are so many wonderful things in our world to enjoy, and yet we concentrate on what is not going well.

Sometimes Thây walks through the kitchen where his disciples are preparing a meal, and he asks someone, "What are you doing, my child?" Thây can see very well that his disciple is washing lettuce or cutting green beans. The aim of the question is not to enlighten Thây as to what someone is doing but to awaken the disciple to the present moment. The answer might be: "Thank you for bringing me back to my true self," or a smile of recognition that we are not in the present moment.

Thây has brought to us in the West some precious jewels from the Asian practice of Buddhism. But he has also reminded us that we have many jewels in our own spiritual traditions which we may have forgotten and which we could revive. Thây records how when he heard the sound of the Angelus bell in Czechoslovakia it brought to him the soul of ancient Europe. He was reminded how in Vietnam it used to be the custom to stop when the temple bell was heard in the village. No doubt the villagers would use those moments to recollect the Buddha. Thây always teaches his students to stop and to breathe when they hear the sound of the bell in the meditation center. No matter what we are doing we use this opportunity to stop and come back to our true self. Since the sound of bells is not available to many of us in our daily life, Thây has suggested we substitute the sound of the telephone ringing. Thây has suggested that we simply breathe when we hear the sound of the bell or the telephone, using the opportunity to come back to our true self. Thus the practice becomes open to everyone, whether Buddhist, Jewish, or Christian.

Thây has often taught that our mind is like a television set with many channels. In the present moment we can choose the channel that we want to watch. Buddha has taught that there are fifty-one mental formations including love, joy, hate, jealousy, feelings, and perceptions, and it is up to us to choose which program we want to watch. For many of us, however, a program will appear on the screen of our mental television which is not of our choosing. This is because we have not yet trained in the art of mindfulness, which is the art of recognizing which mental formation is arising and of taking good care of that mental formation as it arises and for as long as it is present. The more mindful we are the more we can choose which mental formations appear on the screen of our mind.

Thây does not mean to tell us that we should not suffer or that suffering is wrong. Thây has suffered much and would not advise us not to suffer. It is our suffering that makes us compassionate. It is our suffering that acts as compost to bring about the flowers and fruits of understanding and compassion. Thây tells his disciples, *"You have every right to suffer, but you do not have the right not to practice when you suffer." If we do not practice mindful breathing and walking when we suffer, we shall drown in our suffering and it will not be converted into that compost on which the flowers of understanding can grow.*

—Sister Annabel Laity

EACH STEP

Through the deserted gate
full of ripened leaves,
I follow the small path.
Earth is as red as a child's lips.
Suddenly
I am aware
of each step
I make.
— *Call Me by My True Names*

LIFE IS A MIRACLE

In Vietnam when I was a young monk, each village temple had a big bell, like those in Christian churches in Europe and America. Whenever the bell was invited to sound, all the villagers would stop what they were doing and pause for a few moments to breathe in and out in mindfulness. At Plum Village, the community where I live in France, we do the same. Every time we hear the bell, we go back to ourselves and enjoy our breathing. When we breathe in, we say, silently, "Listen, listen," and when we breathe out, we say, "This wonderful sound brings me back to my true home."

Our true home is in the present moment. To live in the present moment is a miracle. The miracle is not to walk on water. The miracle is to walk on the green Earth in the present moment, to appreciate the peace and beauty that are available now. Peace is all around us — in the world and in nature — and within us — in our bodies and our spirits. Once we learn to touch this peace, we will be healed and transformed. It is not a matter of faith; it is a matter of practice. We need only to find ways to bring our body and mind back to the present moment so we can touch what is refreshing, healing, and wondrous.

Last year in New York City, I rode in a taxi, and I saw that the driver was not at all happy. He was not in the present moment. There was no peace or joy in him, no capacity of being alive while doing the work of driving, and he expressed it in the way he drove. Many of us do the same. We rush about, but we are not at one with what we are doing; we are not at peace. Our body is here, but our mind is somewhere else — in the past or the future, possessed by anger, frustration, hopes, or dreams. We are not really alive; we are like ghosts. If our beautiful child were to come up to us and offer us a smile, we would miss him completely, and he would miss us. What a pity!

In *The Stranger,* Albert Camus described a man who was going to be executed in a few days. Sitting alone in his cell, he noticed a small patch of blue sky through the skylight, and suddenly he felt deeply in touch with life, deeply in the present moment. He vowed to live his remaining days in mindfulness, in full appreciation of each moment, and he did so for several days. Then, just three hours before the time of his execution, a priest came into the cell to receive a confession and administer the last rites. But the man wanted only to be alone. He tried many ways to get the priest to leave, and when he finally succeeded, he said to himself that the priest lived like a dead man. *"Il vit comme un mort."* He saw that the one who was trying to save him was less alive than he, the one who was about to be executed.

Many of us, although alive, are not really alive, because we are not able to touch life in the present moment. We are like dead people, as Camus says. I would like to share with you a few simple exercises we can practice that can help us re-unify our body and mind and get back in touch with life in the present moment. The first is called conscious breathing, and human beings like us have been practicing this for more than three thousand years. As we breathe in, we know we are breath-ing in, and as we breathe out, we know we are breathing out. As we do this, we observe many elements of happiness inside us and around us. We can really enjoy touching our breathing and our being alive.

Life is found only in the present moment. I think we should have a holiday to celebrate this fact. We have holidays for so many important occasions — Christmas, New Year's, Mother's Day, Father's Day, even Earth Day — why not celebrate a day when we can live happily in the present moment all day long? I would like to declare today "Today's Day," a day dedicated to touching the Earth, touching the sky, touching the trees, and touching the peace that is available in the present moment.

The best way to touch is with mindfulness. You know, it is possible to touch without mindfulness. When you wash your face in the morning, you might touch your eyes without be-ing aware that you are touching them. You might be thinking about other things. But if you wash your face in mindfulness, aware that you have eyes that can see, that the water comes from distant sources to make washing your face possible, your washing will be much deeper. As you touch your eyes, you can say, "Breathing in, I am aware of my eyes. Breathing out, I smile to my eyes."

Our eyes are refreshing, healing, and peaceful elements that are available to us. We pay so much attention to what is wrong, why not notice what is wonderful and refreshing? We rarely take the time to appreciate our eyes. When we touch our eyes with our hands and our mindfulness, we notice that our eyes are precious jewels that are fundamental for our happiness. Those who have lost their sight feel that if they could see as well as we do, they would be in paradise. We only need to open our eyes, and we see every kind of form and color — the blue sky, the beautiful hills, the trees, the clouds, the rivers, the children, the butterflies. Just sitting here and enjoying these colors and shapes, we can be extremely happy. Seeing is a miracle, a condition for our happiness, yet most of the time we take it for granted. We don't act as if we are in paradise. When we practice breathing in and becoming aware of our eyes, breathing out and smiling to our eyes, we touch real peace and joy.

We can do the same with our heart. "Breathing in, I am aware of my heart. Breathing out, I smile to my heart." If we practice this a few times, we will realize that our heart has been working hard, day and night, for many years to keep us alive. Our heart pumps thousands of gallons of blood every day, without stopping. Even while we sleep, our heart continues its work to bring us peace and well-being. Our heart is an element of peace and joy, but we don't touch or appreciate it. We only touch the things that make us suffer, and because of that, we give our heart a hard time by our worries and strong emotions, and by what we eat and drink. Doing so, we undermine our own peace and joy. When we practice breathing in and becoming aware of our heart, breathing out and smiling to our heart, we become enlightened. We see our heart so clearly. When we smile to our heart, we are massaging it with our compassion. When we know what to eat and what not to eat, what to drink and what not to drink, what worries and despair we should avoid, we will keep our heart safe.

When we have a toothache, we know that not having a toothache is a wonderful thing. "Breathing in, I am aware of my non-toothache. Breathing out, I smile at my non-toothache." We can touch our non-toothache with our mindfulness, and even with our hands. When we have asthma and can hardly breathe, we realize that breathing freely is a wonderful thing. Even when we have just a stuffed nose, we know that breathing freely is a wonderful thing.

Every day we touch what is wrong, and, as a result, we are

becoming less and less healthy. That is why we have to learn to practice touching what is not wrong — inside us and around us. When we get in touch with our eyes, our heart, our liver, our breathing, and our non-toothache and really enjoy them, we see that the conditions for peace and happiness are already present. When we walk mindfully and touch the Earth with our feet, when we drink tea with friends and touch the tea and our friendship, we get healed, and we can bring this healing to society. The more we have suffered in the past, the stronger a healer we can become. We can learn to transform our suffering into the kind of insight that will help our friends and society.

We do not have to die to enter the Kingdom of Heaven. In fact we have to be fully alive. When we breathe in and out and hug a beautiful tree, we are in Heaven. When we take one conscious breath, aware of our eyes, our heart, our liver, and our non-toothache, we are transported to Paradise right away. Peace is available. We only have to touch it. When we are truly alive, we can see that the tree is part of Heaven, and we are also part of Heaven. The whole universe is conspiring to reveal this to us, but we are so out of touch that we invest our resources in cutting down the trees. If we want to enter Heaven on Earth, we need only one conscious step and one conscious breath. When we touch peace, everything becomes real. We become ourselves, fully alive in the present moment, and the tree, our child, and everything else reveal themselves to us in their full splendor.

"The miracle is to walk on Earth." This statement was made by Zen Master Lin Chi. The miracle is not to walk on thin air or water, but to walk on Earth. The Earth is so beautiful. We are beautiful also. We can allow ourselves to walk mindfully, touching the Earth, our wonderful mother, with each step. We don't need to wish our friends, "Peace be with you." Peace is already with them. We only need to help them cultivate the habit of touching peace in each moment.   — *Touching Peace*

SUFFERING IS NOT ENOUGH

Life is filled with suffering, but it is also filled with many wonders, like the blue sky, the sunshine, the eyes of a baby. To suffer is not enough. We must also be in touch with the wonders of life. They are within us and all around us, everywhere, any time.

If we are not happy, if we are not peaceful, we cannot share peace and happiness with others, even those we love, those who live under the same roof. If we are peaceful, if we are happy, we can smile and blossom like a flower, and everyone in our family, our entire society, will benefit from our peace. Do we need to make a special effort to enjoy the beauty of the blue sky? Do we have to practice to be able to enjoy it? No, we just enjoy it. Each second, each minute of our lives can be like this. Wherever we are, any time, we have the capacity to enjoy the sunshine, the presence of each other, even the sensation of our breathing. We don't need to go to China to enjoy the blue sky. We don't have to travel into the future to enjoy our breathing. We can be in touch with these things right now. It would be a pity if we are only aware of suffering.

We are so busy we hardly have time to look at the people we love, even in our own household, and to look at ourselves. Society is organized in a way that even when we have some leisure time, we don't know how to use it to get back in touch with ourselves. We have millions of ways to lose this precious time — we turn on the TV or pick up the telephone, or start the car and go somewhere. We are not used to being with ourselves, and we act as if we don't like ourselves and are trying to escape from ourselves.

Meditation is to be aware of what is going on — in our bodies, in our feelings, in our minds, and in the world. Each day forty thousand children die of hunger. The superpowers now have more than fifty thousand nuclear warheads, enough to destroy our planet many times. Yet the sunrise is beautiful, and the rose that bloomed this morning along the wall is a miracle. Life is both dreadful and wonderful. To practice meditation is to be in touch with both aspects. Please do not think we must be solemn in order to meditate. In fact, to meditate well, we have to smile a lot.

Recently I was sitting with a group of children, and a boy named Tim was smiling beautifully. I said, "Tim, you have a very beautiful smile," and he said, "Thank you." I told him, "You don't have to thank me, I have to thank you. Because of your smile, you make life more beautiful. Instead of saying, 'Thank you,' you should say 'You're welcome.' "

If a child smiles, if an adult smiles, that is very important. If in our daily life we can smile, if we can be peaceful and happy, not only we, but everyone will profit from it. This is the most basic kind of peace work. When I see Tim smiling, I am so happy. If he is aware that he is making other people happy, he can say, "You are welcome."

•

From time to time, to remind ourselves to relax, to be peaceful, we may wish to set aside some time for a retreat, a day of mindfulness, when we can walk slowly, smile, drink tea with a friend, enjoy being together as if we are the happiest people on Earth. This is not a retreat, it is a treat. During walking meditation, during kitchen and garden work, during sitting meditation, all day long, we can practice smiling. At first you may find it difficult to smile, and we have to think about why. Smiling means that we are ourselves, that we have sovereignty over ourselves, that we are not drowned into forgetfulness. This kind of smile can be seen on the faces of Buddhas and bodhisattvas.

I would like to offer one short poem you can recite from time to time, while breathing and smiling.

> *Breathing in, I calm my body.*
> *Breathing out, I smile.*
> *Dwelling in the present moment*
> *I know this is a wonderful moment.*

"Breathing in, I calm my body." This line is like drinking a glass of ice water — you feel the cold, the freshness, permeate your body. When I breathe in and recite this line, I actually feel the breathing calming my body, calming my mind.

"Breathing out, I smile." You know the effect of a smile. A smile can relax hundreds of muscles in your face, and relax your nervous system. A smile makes you master of yourself. That is why Buddhas and bodhisattvas are always smiling. When you smile, you realize the wonder of the smile.

"Dwelling in the present moment." While I sit here, I don't think of somewhere else, of the future or the past. I sit here, and I know where I am. This is very important. We tend to be alive in the future, not now. We say, "Wait until I finish school and get my Ph.D. degree, and then I will be really alive." When we have it, and it's not easy to get, we say to ourselves, "I have to wait until I have a job in order to be *really* alive." And then after the job, a car. After the car, a house. We are not capable of being alive in the present moment. We tend to postpone being alive to the future, the distant future, we don't know when. Now is not the moment to be alive. We may never be alive at all in our entire life. Therefore, the technique, if we have to speak of a technique, is to *be* in the present moment, to be aware that we are here and now, and the only moment to be alive is the present moment.

"I know this is a wonderful moment." This is the only moment that is real. To be here and now, and enjoy the present moment is our most important task. "Calming, Smiling, Present moment Wonderful moment."   — *Being Peace*

SUNSHINE AND GREEN LEAVES

Today three children, two girls and a little boy, came from the village to play with Thanh Thuy. The four of them ran off to play on the hillside behind our house and were gone for about an hour when they returned to ask for something to drink. I took the last bottle of homemade apple juice and gave them each a full glass, serving Thuy last. Since her juice was from the bottom of the bottle, it had some pulp in it. When she noticed the particles, she pouted and refused to drink it. So the four children went back to their games on the hillside, and Thuy had not drunk anything.

Half an hour later, while I was meditating in my room, I heard her calling. Thuy wanted to get herself a glass of cold water, but even on tiptoes she couldn't reach the faucet. I reminded her of the glass of juice on the table and asked her to drink that first. Turning to look at it, she saw that the pulp had settled and the juice looked clear and delicious. She went to the table and took the glass with both hands. After drinking half of it, she put it down and asked, "Is this a different glass, Uncle Monk?" (a common term for Vietnamese children to use when addressing an older monk).

"No," I answered. "It's the same one as before. It sat quietly for a bit, and now it's clear and delicious." Thuy looked at the glass again. "It really is good. Was it meditating like you, Uncle Monk?" I laughed and patted her head. "Let's say that I imitate the apple juice when I sit; that is closer to the truth."

Every night at Thuy's bedtime, I sit in meditation. I let her sleep in the same room, near where I am sitting. We have agreed that while I am sitting, she will go to bed without talking. In that peaceful atmosphere, rest comes easily to her, and she is usually asleep within five or ten minutes. When I finish sitting, I cover her with a blanket.

Thanh Thuy is the child of "boat people." She is not yet four and a half years old. She crossed the seas with her father and arrived in Malaysia in April of last year. Her mother stayed in Vietnam. When her father arrived here in France, he left Thuy with us for several months while he went to Paris to look for a job.

Every night Thanh Thuy sees me sit. I told her that I am "sit-

ting in meditation" without explaining what it means or why I
do it. Every night when she sees me wash my face, put on my
robes, and light a stick of incense to make the room fragrant,
she knows that soon I will begin "meditating." She also knows
that it is time for her to brush her teeth, change into pajamas,
and go quietly to bed. I have never had to remind her.

Without a doubt, Thuy thought that the apple juice was sitting for a while to clear itself, just like her Uncle Monk. "Was
it meditating like you?" I think that Thanh Thuy, not yet four
and a half, understands the meaning of meditation without any
explanation. The apple juice became clear after resting awhile.
In the same way, if we rest in meditation awhile, we too become clear. This clarity refreshes us and gives us strength and
serenity. As we feel ourselves refreshed, our surroundings also
become refreshed. Children like to be near us, not just to get
candy and hear stories. They like to be near us because they can
feel this "freshness."

We can be better than a glass of apple juice. Not only can we
settle peacefully while sitting still, we can also do it while standing, lying down, walking, or even working. What prevents you
from allowing the sun of awareness to shine while you take a
walk, make a cup of tea or coffee, or wash your clothes? When
I first became a student at the Tu Hieu Monastery, I learned to
maintain awareness during all activities — weeding the garden,
raking leaves around the pond, washing dishes in the kitchen.
I practiced mindfulness in the way taught by Zen Master Doc
The in his little manual, *Essentials of the Practice to Apply Each
Day*. According to this small book, we must be fully aware of
all our actions. While waking up we know that we are waking
up; while buttoning our jacket, we know that we are buttoning our jacket; while washing our hands we know that we are
washing our hands. Master Doc The composed short poems for
us to recite while washing our hands or buttoning our jackets
to help us remain firmly rooted in awareness. Here is the poem
he wrote for us to recite while buttoning our jackets:

While buttoning my jacket
I hope that all beings
Will keep their hearts warm
And not lose themselves.

With the aid of verses like this, it is easy for the sun of awareness to shine its light on our physical actions as well as our
thoughts and feelings. When I was a child I often heard my
mother tell my elder sister that a girl must pay attention to her
every movement. I was glad I was a boy who didn't have to
pay attention like that. It was only when I began to practice
meditation that I realized that I had to pay a thousand times
more attention to my movements than my sister had. And not
only to my movements, but also to my thoughts and feelings!
My mother, like all mothers, knew that a girl who pays attention to her movements becomes more beautiful. Her movements
are not jerky, rushed, or clumsy; they become gentle, calm,
and graceful. Without knowing it, my mother taught my sister
meditation.

In the same way, someone who practices awareness becomes
beautiful to see. A Zen master, observing a student ringing the
bell, sweeping the yard, setting the table, can guess how ripe
that student is, can measure the student's "level of meditation"
in his or her manners and personality. This "level" is the fruit
of the practice of awareness, and the master calls it "the flavor
of Zen."

The secret of meditation is to be conscious of each second
of your existence and to keep the sun of awareness continually
shining — in both the physical and psychological realms, in all
circumstances, on each thing that arises. While drinking a cup
of tea, our mind must be fully present in the act of drinking
the tea. Drinking tea or coffee can be one of our daily pleasures
if we partake of it fully. How much time do you set aside for
one cup of tea? In coffee shops in New York or Tokyo, people
come in, order their coffee, drink it quickly, pay, and rush out

to do something else. This takes a few minutes at most. Often there is loud music playing, and your ears hear the music, your eyes watch others gulping down their coffee, and your mind is thinking of what to do next. You can't really call this drinking coffee.

Have you ever participated in a tea ceremony? It may take two or three hours just being together and drinking one or two cups of tea. The time is not spent talking — only being together and drinking tea. Perhaps you think this is irresponsible because the participants are not worrying about the world situation, but you must admit that people who spend their time this way know how to drink tea, know the pleasure of having tea with a friend.

Devoting two hours to a cup of tea is, I agree, a little extreme. There are many other things to do: gardening, laundry, washing dishes, binding books, writing. Perhaps these other tasks are less pleasant than drinking tea or walking in the hills, but if we do them in full awareness, we will find them quite agreeable. Even washing the dishes after a big meal can be a joy.

•

To my mind, the idea that doing dishes is unpleasant can occur only when you aren't doing them. Once you are standing in front of the sink with your sleeves rolled up and your hands in warm water, it really isn't so bad. I enjoy taking my time with each dish, being fully aware of the dish, the water, and each movement of my hands. I know that if I hurry in order to go and have a cup of tea, the time will be unpleasant, and not worth living. That would be a pity, for each minute, each second of life is a miracle. The dishes themselves and the fact that I am here washing them are miracles! Each bowl I wash, each poem I compose, each time I invite a bell to sound is a miracle, and each has exactly the same value. One day, while washing a bowl, I felt that my movements were as sacred and respectful as bathing a newborn Buddha. If he were to read this, that newborn Buddha would certainly be happy for me, and not at all insulted at being compared with a bowl.

Each thought, each action in the sunlight of awareness becomes sacred. In this light, no boundary exists between the sacred and the profane. I must confess it takes me a bit longer to do the dishes, but I live fully in every moment, and I am happy. Washing the dishes is at the same time a means and an end — that is, not only do we do the dishes in order to have clean dishes, we also do the dishes to live fully in each moment while washing them.

If I am incapable of washing dishes joyfully, if I want to finish them quickly so I can go and have a cup of tea, I will be equally incapable of drinking the tea joyfully. With the cup in my hands I will be thinking about what to do next, and the fragrance and the flavor of the tea, together with the pleasure of drinking it, will be lost. I will always be dragged into the future, never able to live in the present moment.

•

We lead extremely busy lives. Even though we do not have to do as much manual labor as people in former times, we never seem to have enough time for ourselves. I know people who say they do not even have enough time to eat or breathe, and it appears to me to be true! What can we do about this? Can we take hold of time with both hands and slow it down?

First, let us light the torch of our awareness and learn again how to drink tea, eat, wash dishes, walk, sit, drive, and work in awareness. We do not have to be swept along by circumstances. We are not just a leaf or a log in a rushing river. With awareness, each of our daily acts takes on a new meaning, and we discover that we are more than machines, that our activities are not just mindless repetitions. We find that life is a miracle, the universe is a miracle, and we too are a miracle.

— *The Sun My Heart*

GREETING SOMEONE

A lotus for you,
a Buddha to be.

The tradition of joining our palms together and bowing when we meet someone is very beautiful. Millions of men and women in Asia greet each other this way every day. When someone offers me a cup of tea, I always bow respectfully. As I join my palms, I breathe in and say, "A lotus for you." As I bow, I breathe out and say, "A Buddha to be." To join our palms in a lotus bud is to offer the person standing before us a fresh flower. But we have to remember not to join our palms mechanically. We must be aware of the person we are greeting. When our respect is sincere, we remember that he or she has the nature of a Buddha, the nature of awakening.

It is necessary for us to see the Buddha in the person before us. If we practice this way regularly, we will see a change in ourselves. We will develop humility, and we will also realize that our abilities are boundless. When we know how to respect others, we also know how to respect ourselves.

As I bow, mindfulness becomes real in me. Seeing my deep reverence, the person to whom I bow also becomes awake, and he or she may like to form a lotus and bow to me, breathing in and out. With one greeting, mindfulness becomes present in both of us as we touch the Buddha with our hearts, not just with our hands. Suddenly, the Buddha in each of us begins to shine, and we are in touch with the present moment.

Sometimes we think that we are superior to others — perhaps more educated or intelligent. Seeing an uneducated person, a feeling of disdain may arise, but this attitude does not help anyone. Our knowledge is relative and limited. An orchid, for example, knows how to produce noble, symmetrical flowers, and a snail knows how to make a beautiful, well-proportioned shell. Compared with this kind of knowledge, our knowledge is not worth boasting about, even if we have a Ph.D. We should bow deeply before the orchid and the snail and join our palms reverently before the monarch butterfly and the magnolia tree. Feeling respect for all species of living beings and inanimate objects will help us recognize a part of the Buddha nature in ourselves.

In the West, you may prefer to shake hands. But if you greet others mindfully and respectfully, whatever form you use, the Buddha is present.

— Present Moment Wonderful Moment

WALKING MEDITATION

Walking meditation can be very enjoyable. We walk slowly, alone or with friends, if possible in some beautiful place. Walking meditation is really to enjoy the walking — walking not in order to arrive, just for walking. The purpose is to be in the present moment and enjoy each step you make. Therefore you have to shake off all worries and anxieties, not thinking of the future, not thinking of the past, just enjoying the present moment. You can take the hand of a child as you walk, as if you are the happiest person on Earth. We walk all the time, but usually it is more like running. Our hurried steps print anxiety and sorrow on the Earth. If we can take one step in peace, we can take two, three, four, and then five steps for the peace and happiness of humankind.

Our mind darts from one thing to another, like a monkey swinging from branch to branch without stopping to rest. Thoughts have millions of pathways, and we are forever pulled along by them into the world of forgetfulness. If we can transform our walking path into a field for meditation, our feet will take every step in full awareness. Our breathing will be in harmony with our steps, and our mind will naturally be at ease. Every step we take will reinforce our peace and joy and cause a stream of calm energy to flow through us. Then we can say, "With each step, a gentle wind blows."

The Buddha is often represented by artists as seated upon a lotus flower to suggest the peace and happiness he enjoys. Artists also depict lotus flowers blooming under the footsteps of the newly-born Buddha. If we take steps without anxiety, in peace and joy, then we, too, will cause a flower to bloom on the Earth with every step.

— *Present Moment Wonderful Moment*

A TANGERINE PARTY

Yesterday, in our retreat, we had a tangerine party. Everyone was offered one tangerine. We put the tangerine on the palm of our hand and looked at it, breathing in a way that the tangerine became real. Most of the time when we eat a tangerine, we do not look at it. We think about many other things. To look at a tangerine is to see the blossom forming into the fruit, to see the sunshine and the rain. The tangerine in our palm is the wonderful presence of life. We are able to really see that tangerine and smell its blossom and the warm, moist earth. As the tangerine becomes real, we become real. Life in that moment becomes real.

Mindfully we began to peel our tangerine and smell its fragrance. We carefully took each section of the tangerine and put it on our tongue, and we could feel that it was a real tangerine. We ate each section of the tangerine in perfect mindfulness until we finished the entire fruit. Eating a tangerine in this way is very important, because both the tangerine and the eater of the tangerine become real. This, too, is the basic work for peace.

In Buddhist meditation we do not struggle for the kind of enlightenment that will happen five or ten years from now. We practice so that each moment of our life becomes real life. And, therefore, when we meditate, we sit for sitting; we don't sit for something else. If we sit for twenty minutes, these twenty minutes should bring us joy, life. If we practice walking meditation, we walk just for walking, not to arrive. We have to be alive with each step, and if we are, each step brings real life back to us. The same kind of mindfulness can be practiced when we eat breakfast, or when we hold a child in our arms. Hugging is a Western custom, but we from the East would like to contribute the practice of conscious breathing to it. When you hold a child in your arms, or hug your mother, or your husband, or your friend, breathe in and out three times and your happiness will be multiplied by at least tenfold. And when you look at someone, really look at them with mindfulness, and practice conscious breathing.

At the beginning of each meal, I recommend that you look at your plate and silently recite, "My plate is empty now, but I know that it is going to be filled with delicious food in just a moment." While waiting to be served or to serve yourself, I suggest you breathe three times and look at it even more deeply. "At this very moment many, many people around the world are also holding a plate, but their plate is going to be empty for a long time." Forty thousand children die each day because of the lack of food. Children alone. We can be very happy to have such wonderful food, but we also suffer because we are capable of seeing. But when we see in this way, it makes us sane, because the way in front of us is clear — the way to live so that we can make peace with ourselves and with the world. When we see the good and the bad, the wondrous and the deep suffering, we have to live in a way that we can make peace between ourselves and the world. Understanding is the fruit of meditation. Understanding is the basis of everything.

Each breath we take, each step we make, each smile we realize, is a positive contribution to peace, a necessary step in the direction of peace for the world. In the light of interbeing, peace and happiness in your daily life means peace and happiness in the world.   — *The Heart of Understanding*

THE SUN OF AWARENESS

One evening I returned to my hermitage from a walk in the hills, and I found that all the doors and windows of the hermitage had been blown open. When I left the house, I hadn't secured them, and a cold wind blew through the house, opened the windows, and scattered the papers from the desk all over the room. Immediately I closed the doors and windows, lit a lamp, picked up the papers, and arranged them neatly on my desk. Then I started a fire in the fireplace, and soon the crackling logs brought warmth back to the room.

Sometimes in a crowd we feel tired, cold, and lonely. We may wish to withdraw to be by ourselves and become warm again, as I did at the hermitage sitting by the fire, protected from the cold, damp wind. Our senses are our windows to the outside world, and sometimes the wind blows and disturbs everything within us. Many of us leave our windows open all the time, allowing the sights and sounds of the world to invade us, penetrate us, and expose our sad, troubled selves. We feel so cold and lonely and afraid. Do you ever find yourself watching an awful TV program, unable to turn it off? The raucous noises, explosions of gunfire, are upsetting. Yet you don't get up and turn it off. Why do you torture yourself in this way? Don't you want to close your windows? Are you afraid of solitude — the emptiness and the loneliness you may find when you face yourself alone?

We are what we feel and perceive. If we are angry, we are the anger. If we are in love, we are the love. If we look at a snowy mountain peak, we are the mountain. Watching a bad TV program, we are the TV program. While dreaming, we are the dream. We can be anything we want, even without a magic wand. So why do we open our windows to bad movies and TV programs, movies made by sensationalist producers in search of easy money, movies which make our hearts pound, our fists tighten, and send us back into the streets exhausted? Who allows such movies and TV programs to be made? Especially for the very young. We do! We are too undemanding, too ready to watch whatever is on the screen, too lonely, lazy, or bored to create our own lives. We turn on the TV and leave it on, allowing someone else to guide us, shape us, and destroy us. Losing ourselves in this way is leaving our fate in the hands of others who may not be acting responsibly. We must be aware of what kinds of programs do harm to our nervous systems, our minds, and our hearts, and which programs and films benefit us.

I am not just talking about movies and TV programs. All around us, how many lures are set there by our fellows and ourselves? In a single day, how many times do we become lost and scattered because of them? We must be very careful to protect our fate and our peace. That does not mean shutting all our windows, for there are many miracles in the world we call "outside." Open your windows to these miracles. Look at any one of them with the light of awareness. Even while sitting beside a clear, flowing stream listening to beautiful music, or watching an excellent movie, do not entrust yourself entirely to the stream, the music, or the film. Continue to be aware of yourself and your breathing. With the sun of awareness shining in us, we can avoid most dangers — the stream will be purer, the music more harmonious, and the soul of the artist completely visible in the film.

Around us, life bursts forth with miracles — a glass of water, a ray of sunshine, a leaf, a caterpillar, a flower, laughter, raindrops. If you live in awareness, it is easy to see miracles everywhere. Each human being is a multiplicity of miracles. Eyes that see thousands of colors, shapes, and forms; ears that hear a bee flying or a thunderclap; a brain that ponders a speck of dust as easily as the entire cosmos; a heart that beats in rhythm with the heartbeat of all beings. When we are tired and feel discouraged by life's daily struggles, we may not notice these miracles, but they are always there.

Have a look at the apple tree in your yard. Look at it with

complete attention. It is truly a miracle. If you notice it, you will take good care of it, and you too are part of its miraculousness. Even after caring for it for only a week, its leaves are already greener and shinier. It is exactly the same with the people who are around you. Under the influence of awareness, you become more attentive, understanding, and loving, and your presence not only nourishes you and makes you lovelier, it enhances them as well. Our entire society can be changed by one person's peaceful presence.

Our minds create everything. The majestic mountain top, brilliant with snow, is you yourself when you contemplate it. Its existence depends on your awareness. When you close your eyes, as long as your mind is present, the mountain is there. Sitting in meditation, with several sense-windows closed, you feel the presence of the whole universe. Why? Because the mind is there. If your eyes are closed, it is so that you can see better. The sights and sounds of the world are not your "enemies." Your "enemy" is forgetfulness, the absence of mindfulness.

— *The Sun My Heart*

MENTAL FORMATIONS

If we live in forgetfulness, if we lose ourselves in the past or in the future, if we allow ourselves to be tossed about by our desires, anger, and ignorance, we will not be able to live each moment of our life deeply. We will not be in contact with what is happening in the present moment, and our relations with others will become shallow and impoverished.

Some days we may feel hollow, exhausted, and joyless, not really our true selves. On such days, even if we try to be in touch with others, our efforts will be in vain. The more we try, the more we fail. When this happens, we should stop trying to be in touch with what is outside of ourselves and come back to being in touch with ourselves, to "being alone." We should close the door onto society, come back to ourselves, and practice conscious breathing, observing deeply what is going on inside and around us. We accept all the phenomena we observe, say "hello" to them, smile at them. We do well to do simple things, like walking or sitting meditation, washing our clothes, cleaning the floor, making tea, and cleaning the bathroom in mindfulness. If we do these things, we will restore the richness of our spiritual life.

Buddha taught that we should not pursue the past "because the past no longer is." When we are lost in thoughts about the past, we lose the present. Life exists only in the present moment. To lose the present is to lose life. The Buddha's meaning is very clear: we must say good-bye to the past so that we may return to the present. To return to the present is to be in touch with life.

What dynamics in our consciousness compel us to go back and live with the images of the past? These forces are made up of internal formations, mental factors which arise in us and bind us. Things we see, hear, smell, taste, touch, imagine, or think can all give rise to internal formations — desire, irritation, anger, confusion, fear, anxiety, suspicion, and so on. Internal formations are present in the depths of the consciousness of each of us.

Internal formations influence our consciousness and our everyday behavior. They cause us to think, say, and do things that we may not even be aware of. Because they compel us in this way, they are also called fetters, because they bind us to acting in certain ways.

•

The present contains the past. When we understand how our internal formations cause conflicts in us, we can see how the past is in the present moment, and we will no longer be overwhelmed by the past. When the Buddha said, "Do not pursue the past," he was telling us not to be overwhelmed by the past.

He did not mean that we should stop looking at the past in order to observe it deeply. When we review the past and observe it deeply, if we are standing firmly in the present, we are not overwhelmed by it. The materials of the past which make up the present become clear when they express themselves in the present. We can learn from them. If we observe these materials deeply, we can arrive at a new understanding of them. That is called "looking again at something old in order to learn something new."

If we know that the past also lies in the present, we understand that we are able to change the past by transforming the present. The ghosts of the past, which follow us into the present, also belong to the present moment. To observe them deeply, recognize their nature, and transform them, is to transform the past. The ghosts of the past are very real. They are the internal formations in us which are sometimes quietly asleep, while at other times they awaken suddenly and act in a strong way.

Sometimes, because the present is so difficult, we give our attention to the future, hoping that the situation will improve in the future. Imagining the future will be better, we are better able to accept the suffering and hardship of the present. But at other times, thinking about the future may cause us a lot of fear and anxiety, and yet we cannot stop doing it. The reason we continue to think about the future, even when we do not want to, is due to the presence of internal formations. Although not yet here, the future is already producing ghosts which haunt us. In fact, these ghosts are not produced by the future or the past. It is our consciousness which creates them. The past and the future are creations of our consciousness.

To return to the present moment is to discover life and to realize the truth. All the Awakened Ones of the past have come to Awakening in the present moment. All the Awakened Ones of the present and the future will realize the fruit of Awakening in the present also. Only the present moment is real.

If we do not stand firmly in the present moment, we may feel ungrounded when we look at the future. We may think that in the future we will be alone, with no place of refuge and no one to help us. Such concerns about the future bring about unease, anxiety, and fear, and do not help us at all in taking care of the present moment. They just make our way of dealing with the present weak and confused. The best way of preparing for the future is to take good care of the present, because we know that if the present is made up of the past, then the future will be made up of the present. All we need to be responsible for is the present moment. Only the present is within our reach. To care for the present is to care for the future.

To return to the present is to be in contact with life. Life can be found only in the present moment, because "the past no longer is" and "the future has not yet come." Buddhahood, liberation, awakening, peace, joy, and happiness can only be found in the present moment. Our appointment with life is in the present moment. The place of our appointment is right here, in this very place.

In Buddhism, "aimlessness" is taught as a way to help the practitioner stop pursuing the future and return wholly to the present. To be able to stop pursuing the future allows us to realize that all the wonderful things we seek are present in us, in the present moment. Life is not a particular place or a destination. Life is a path. To practice walking meditation is to go without needing to arrive. Every step can bring us peace, joy, and liberation. That is why we walk in the spirit of aimlessness. There is no way to liberation, peace, and joy; peace and joy are themselves the way. Our appointment with the Buddha, with liberation, and with happiness is here and now. We should not miss this appointment.   — *Our Appointment with Life*

TOUCHING THE ULTIMATE DIMENSION

Seven years after the death of my mother, I woke up suddenly one night, went outside, and saw the moon shining brightly. At two or three o'clock in the morning, the moon is always expressing something deep, calm, and tender, like the love of a mother for her child. I felt bathed in her love, and I realized that my mother is still alive and will always be alive. A few hours earlier, I had seen my mother very clearly in a dream. She was young and beautiful, talking to me, and I talked to her. Since that time, I know that my mother is always with me. She pretended to die, but it is not true. Our mothers and fathers continue in us. Our liberation is their liberation. Whatever we do for our transformation is also for their transformation, and for our children and their children.

When you touch the present moment, you touch the past and the future. When you touch time, you touch space. When you touch space, you touch time. When you touch the lemon tree in early spring, you touch the lemons that will be there in three or four months. You can do that because the lemons are already there. You can touch the lemon tree in the historical dimension or the ultimate dimension; it is up to you.

When you touch the wave, you touch the water at the same time. That is our practice. If you are with a group of friends practicing mindfulness while sitting, walking, or drinking tea, you will be able to touch the ultimate dimension while living in the historical dimension. Your fear, anxiety, and anger will be transformed easily when you are not confined by the waves, when you are able to touch the water at the same time.

The world of peace and joy is at our fingertips. We only need to touch it. When I enter the Plum Village kitchen, I may ask a student, "What are you doing?" If she says, "Thây, I am cutting some carrots," I will feel a little disappointed. I want her to leave the historical dimension and touch the ultimate dimension. She only needs to look up and smile. Or if she was thinking of something else and was brought back to the present moment by my question, she might look up and say, "Thank you," or "I am breathing." Those are good answers. You do not have to die to enter the Kingdom of God. In fact, you have to be alive to do so. What makes you alive? Mindfulness. Everything around you and in you can be the door to enter the *Dharmadhatu*.

When I was a little boy, I read a novel about a French hunter who got lost in an African jungle. He thought that he was going to die, because he could not find his way out. But he was adamant that he would not pray to God. So he did something that was half-praying and half-joking: *"Dieu, si tu existes, viens à mon secours!"* (God, if you exist, come and rescue me!) A few minutes later, an African showed himself and helped him out. Later he wrote, *"J'ai appelé Dieu, et il est arrivé un nègre."* (I called God, but a Negro came.) He did not know that the African *was* God. We might be saved by a flower, a pebble, a bird, or a thunderclap. Anything can bring us a message from Heaven. Anything can wake us up to life right here and right now. We should not discriminate.

We have within us a miraculous power, and if we live our daily lives in mindfulness, if we take steps mindfully, with love and care, we can produce the miracle and transform our world into a miraculous place to live. Taking steps slowly, in mindfulness, is an act of liberation. You walk and you free yourself of all worries, anxieties, projects, and attachments. One step like this has the power to liberate you from all afflictions. Just being there, you transform yourself, and your compassion will bear witness. — *Cultivating the Mind of Love*

REAL HEROES

In former days, my friends and I wanted to become heroes who could "shatter misfortune and level calamity." We did not know what it takes to become a hero, so we tried to imitate the knights of old. I cannot help smiling when I think of our youthful dreams. We hardly looked the part of brave knights as we clutched our bamboo swords and repeated the words of the ancients. Now as I write, surrounded by a cold and bustling city, I feel a bit of the old desire. The world is the same as when we were children, still patiently awaiting the appearance of real heroes.

Before the knights of old descended their mountain training grounds to rescue those in need, they trained a long time with revered masters in the martial arts. My training as a Buddhist novice consisted of one small book, *Gathas for Daily Life*. I learned to cook, sweep, carry water, and chop wood. Some of us did not have enough time to learn the arts of cooking, sweeping, carrying water, and chopping wood before being forced to descend the mountain. Others descended of their own will before they were ready. With our talents and abilities still undeveloped, how could we save others? We may have thought of ourselves as heroic, indispensable, and may even have called ourselves heroes, but society too often accepts those who are heroes in appearance only, making it possible for such people to think they are true heroes. They come to believe that if they were not present, everything would fall apart. And yet when my friends and I left Phuong Boi, the world did not disintegrate.

Life waits patiently for true heroes. It is dangerous when those aspiring to be heroes cannot wait until they find themselves. When aspiring heroes have not found themselves, they are tempted to borrow the world's weapons — money, fame, and power — to fight their battles. These weapons cannot protect the inner life of the hero. To cope with his fears and insecurities, the premature hero has to stay busy all the time. The destructive capacity of nonstop busyness rivals nuclear weapons and is as addictive as opium. It empties the life of the spirit. False heroes find it easier to make war than deal with the emptiness in their own souls. They may complain about never having time to rest, but the truth is, if they were given time to rest, they would not know what to do. People today do not know how to rest. They fill their free time with countless diversions. People cannot tolerate even a few minutes of unoccupied time. They have to turn on the TV or pick up a newspaper, reading anything at all, even the advertisements. They constantly need something to look at, listen to, or talk about, all to keep the emptiness inside from rearing its terrifying head.

When I was a child, I read a funny story about a man who always boasted to his friends about his brave exploits. But at home he was so afraid of his wife, he did not dare look at her crosswise. Present-day heroes are like that. They think they are real heroes because they are so busy, but if we could see their inner lives, we would see desolation. Present-day heroes descend the mountain intending to transform life, but are instead overcome by life. Without fierce resolve and a mature spiritual life, private demons cannot be controlled.

Gathas for Daily Life was a warrior's manual on strategy. As novices, we were handed it when we entered the monastery and instructed to keep it close at hand at all times, even to use it as a pillow at night. The verses in it taught us how to stay present with our own minds in order to observe ourselves throughout the ordinary actions of daily life: eating, drinking, walking, standing, lying down, and working. It was as difficult as trying to find a stray water buffalo by following its zigzagging tracks. It is not easy to follow the path of return to your own mind. The mind is like a monkey swinging from branch to branch. It is not easy to catch a monkey. You have to be quick and smart, able to guess which branch the monkey will swing to next. It would be easy to shoot it, but the object here is not to kill, threaten, or coerce the monkey. The object is to know where it will go next in order to be with it. That thin book of daily verses provided us with strategies. The verses were simple, yet remarkably effective. They taught us how to observe and master all the actions of body, speech, and mind. For instance, when we washed our hands, we said to ourselves:

> *Washing my hands in clear water,*
> *I pray that all people have pure hands*
> *to receive and care for the truth.*

The use of such *gathas* encourages clarity and mindfulness, making even the most ordinary tasks sacred. Going to the bathroom, taking out the garbage, and chopping wood become acts infused with poetry and art.

Even if you have the perseverance to sit for nine years facing a wall, sitting is only one part of Zen. While cooking, washing dishes, sweeping, carrying water, or chopping wood, you dwell deeply in the present moment. We don't cook in order to have food to eat. We don't wash dishes to have clean dishes. We cook to cook, and we wash dishes to wash dishes. The purpose is not to get these chores out of the way in order to do something more meaningful. Washing the dishes and cooking are themselves the path to Buddhahood. Buddhahood does not come from long hours of sitting. The practice of Zen is to eat, breathe, cook, carry water, and scrub the toilet — to infuse every act of body, speech, and mind — with mindfulness, to illuminate every leaf and pebble, every heap of garbage, every path that leads to our mind's return home. Only a person who has grasped the art of cooking, washing dishes, sweeping, and chopping wood, someone who is able to laugh at the world's weapons of money, fame, and power, can hope to descend the mountain as a hero. A hero like that will traverse the waves of success and failure without rising or sinking. In fact, few people will recognize him as a hero at all.

— *Fragrant Palm Leaves*

EYES OF MINDFULNESS

In our time, the struggle between old and new will reach its
crescendo. It's not over yet, and we carry scars of this struggle
in our hearts. Questions raised by contemporary philosophers
make us feel lost and anxious. Confused minds suggest that existence is meaningless, even absurd, and this adds another coat
of black to our darkened hearts. "Existence is foul. Humans are
loathsome. No one can hope to be good. There is no way to
beautify life." Even while adopting such mindsets, people cling
to the illusion that we are free to be who we want. Yet most
of the time we are merely reacting to the wounds engraved on
our hearts or acting out of our collective karma. Almost no one
listens to his or her true self. But when we are not ourselves,
any freedom we think we have is illusory. Sometimes we reject
freedom because we fear it. Our true selves are buried beneath
layers of moss and brick. We have to break through those layers and be liberated, but we are afraid it may break us, also. We
have to remind ourselves over and over again that the layers of
moss and brick are not our true selves.

When you realize that, you'll see every phenomenon, every
Dharma, with new eyes. Begin by looking deeply at yourself and
seeing how miraculous your body is. There is never any reason
to look at your physical body with contempt or disregard. Don't
ignore the very things that lie within your grasp. We don't value
them. We even curse them. Consider your eyes. How can we
take something as wonderful as our eyes for granted? Yet we
do. We don't look deeply at these wonders. We ignore them,
and, as a result, we lose them. It's as though our eyes don't
exist. Only when we are struck blind do we realize how precious our eyes were, and then it's too late. A blind person who
regains her sight understands the preciousness of her eyes. She
has the capacity to live happily right here on Earth. The world
of form and color is a miracle that offers blissful joys every day.
After we have this realization, we cannot look at the blue sky

and the white clouds without smiling. The world constantly reveals its freshness and splendor. A blind person who regains her sight knows that paradise is right here, but before long she too will start to take it for granted again. Paradise comes to seem commonplace, and, in a matter of weeks or months, she'll lose the realization that she is in paradise. But when our "spiritual eyes" are opened, we never lose the ability to see the wonder of all dharmas, all things.

When I was a young monk I was taught that the greatest sufferings were birth, sickness, old age, death, unfulfilled dreams, separation from loved ones, and contact with those we despise. But the real suffering of humankind lies in the way we look at reality. Look, and you will see that birth, old age, sickness, death, unfulfilled hopes, separation from loved ones, and contact with those we despise are also wonders in themselves. They are all precious aspects of existence. Without them, existence would not be possible. Most important is knowing how to ride the waves of impermanence, smiling as one who knows he has never been born and will never die.

The Buddha told this story: "A man threw a stone at a dog. Crazed with pain, the dog barked at the stone, not understanding that the cause of his pain was the man, not the stone." In the same way, we think that forms, sounds, smells, tastes, and objects of touch are the sources of our suffering, and that to overcome suffering, form, sound, smell, taste, and touch must all be destroyed. We don't realize that our suffering lies in the way we see and use form, sound, smell, taste, and touch, because we view reality through the dark curtains of our narrow views and selfish desires.

Here in America, I feel an intense longing for the familiar sound of Vietnamese. There are times I think, If I could only hear a familiar voice for two minutes, I could be happy all day long. One morning Phuong telephoned. It seemed completely natural to be talking to him. Though we didn't talk long, I was in good spirits the rest of the day.

Since then, whenever I talk with a friend, I listen with all my attention to their words and the tone of their voice. As a result, I hear their worries, dreams, and hopes. It is not easy to listen so deeply that you understand everything the other person is trying to tell you. But every one of us can cultivate the capacity of listening deeply. I am no longer indifferent to phenomena that pass before my senses. A leaf, a child's voice — these are the treasures of life. I look and listen deeply in order to receive the messages these miracles convey. Separation from loved ones, disappointments, impatience with unpleasant things — all these are also constructive and wonderful. Who we are is, in part, a result of our unpleasant experiences. Deep looking allows us to see the wondrous elements contained in the weaknesses of others and ourselves, and these flowers of insight will never wilt. With insight, we see that the world of birth and death and the world of nirvana are the same. One night while practicing sitting meditation I felt the urge to shout, "The work of all the Buddhas has been completely fulfilled!"

It is not possible to judge any event as simply fortunate or unfortunate, good or bad. It is like the old story about the farmer and the horse.* You must travel throughout all of time and space to know the true impact of any event. Every success contains some difficulties, and every failure contributes to increased wisdom or future success. Every event is both fortunate and unfortunate. Fortunate and unfortunate, good and bad, exist only in our perceptions.

People think it is impossible to establish a system of ethics without referring to good or evil. But clouds float, flowers bloom, and wind blows. What need have they for a distinction

---

*One day a farmer went to the field and found that his horse had run away. The people in the village told the farmer it was "bad luck." The next day the horse returned and the village people said, "That is good luck!" Then the farmer's son fell off the horse and broke his leg. The villagers told the farmer that this was bad luck. Soon after, a war broke out and young men from the village were being drafted. But because the farmer's son had a broken leg, he was not drafted. Now the village people told the farmer that his son's broken leg was really "good luck."

between good and evil? There are people who live like clouds, flowers, and wind, who don't think about morals, yet many people point to their actions and words as religious and ethical models, and they praise them as saints. These saints simply smile. If they revealed that they do not know what is good and what is evil, people would think they were crazy.

Who is the real poet? The sweet dew that a real poet drinks every day might poison others. For someone who has seen into the nature of things, knowledge gives rise to action. For those who have truly seen, there is no philosophy of action needed. There is no knowledge, attainment, or object of attainment. Life is lived just as the wind blows, clouds drift, and flowers bloom. When you know how to fly you don't need a street map. Your language is the language of clouds, wind, and flowers. If asked a philosophical question, you might answer with a poem, or ask, "Have you had your breakfast? Then please wash your bowl." Or point to the mountain forest.

If you don't believe me, look and see.
Autumn has arrived.
Scattered leaves of many colors
flood the mountain forest!

If they still cannot see, you might pick up a stick and threaten to strike them in order to get them to stop using concepts to try to understand the truth.

In fifteen minutes, it will be midnight. Christmas is almost here. I am awake in this sacred hour writing in my journal. My thoughts flow, and it feels wonderful to pour them onto paper. I've written about the spiritual experience that revealed to me how to look and listen with full attention. Such moments might only come once in a lifetime. They appear as ambassadors of truth, messengers from reality. If we're not mindful, they may pass unnoticed. The secret of Zen masters is discovering the path of return to such moments, and knowing how to pave the way for such moments to arise. The masters know how to use the dazzling light of those moments to illuminate the journey of return, the journey that begins from nowhere and has no destination.   — *Fragrant Palm Leaves*

JOURNEY

Here are words written down —
footprints on the sand,
cloud formations.

Tomorrow
I'll be gone.
    — *Call Me by My True Names*

2

The Sun My Heart

The teachings of interdependence, of interbeing, and interpenetration — that the one is the all and the all are the one — are some of the deepest teachings of Buddhism, though they are not easily understood. I always thought that understanding these teachings was the result of insight that could be achieved only after decades of concentration. From Thây I learned that once we have the capacity to dwell in the present moment with the help of our conscious breathing and awareness, we can immediately look deeply into the nature of all that is.

Before I met Thây I had struggled for years trying to understand the Prajnaparamita Heart Sutra. *I had read many commentaries, which only left me more confused. When, at a retreat in England in 1986, I first heard Thây teach about the interbeing nature of a piece of paper, I was astounded. How could something which had always sounded so complex and had inspired thousands of pages of commentary turn out to be so simple? Thây simply held up a white sheet of paper and told us what its nature was, how it did not have a separate self, but was just a composite of different causes and conditions including the clouds, the sunshine, the Earth, and the bread which the logger ate. Thây asked us, "Can you see the cloud in this piece of paper?" It was so simple that even a young child could understand. Yet, as Thây spoke, there was a deeper transmission, a* connection of energy between Thây and the audience, so that the interbeing nature of the piece of paper was something that went beyond words.

The same thing happened early one morning in 1988 when I was standing in Bodhgaya with Thây gazing at the red ball of fire which we call the rising sun. Thây told me to take a look at the sun: That sun is your heart, he said. It is your heart because without the sun you would not be alive. The sun is not outside of the lettuce and the sun is not outside of you. We often stop to enjoy the magnificence of the sunset or the sunrise. Looking at the sun at these times does not hurt our eyes, and these are moments when we dwell in the present moment and we can smile to the sun and feel how our life and the life of the sun "inter-are." This is insight and it is not theory. The insight is born when we are really present.

—Sister Annabel Laity

INTERBEING

The sun has entered me.
The sun has entered me together with the cloud
and the river.
I myself have entered the river,
and I have entered the sun
with the cloud and the river.
There has not been a moment
when we do not interpenetrate.

But before the sun entered me,
the sun was in me —
also the cloud and the river.
Before I entered the river,
I was already in it.

There has not been a moment
When we have not *inter-been.*

Therefore you know
that as long as you continue to breathe,
I continue to be in you.
                    — *Call Me by My True Names*

If you are a poet, you will see clearly that there is a cloud floating in this sheet of paper. Without a cloud, there will be no rain;
without rain, the trees cannot grow; and without trees, we cannot make paper. The cloud is essential for the paper to exist. If
the cloud is not here, the sheet of paper cannot be here either.
So we can say that the cloud and the paper *inter-are.* "Interbeing" is a word that is not in the dictionary yet, but if we
combine the prefix "inter" with the verb "to be," we have a
new verb, inter-be. Without a cloud, we cannot have paper, so
we can say that the cloud and the sheet of paper *inter-are.*

If we look into this sheet of paper even more deeply, we can
see the sunshine in it. If the sunshine is not there, the forest
cannot grow. In fact, nothing can grow. Even we cannot grow
without sunshine. And so, we know that the sunshine is also in
this sheet of paper. The paper and the sunshine inter-are. And
if we continue to look, we can see the logger who cut the tree
and brought it to the mill to be transformed into paper. And we
see the wheat. We know that the logger cannot exist without his
daily bread, and therefore, the wheat that became his bread is
also in this sheet of paper. And the logger's father and mother
are in it too. When we look in this way, we see that without all
of these things, this sheet of paper cannot exist.

Looking even more deeply, we can see we are in it too. This
is not difficult to see, because when we look at a sheet of paper,
the sheet of paper is part of our perception. Your mind is in here
and mine is also. So we can say that everything is in here with
this sheet of paper. You cannot point out one thing that is not

here — time, space, the Earth, the rain, the minerals in the soil, the sunshine, the cloud, the river, the heat. Everything co-exists with this sheet of paper. That is why I think the word "inter-be" should be in the dictionary. "To be" is to inter-be. You cannot just *be* by yourself alone. You have to inter-be with every other thing. This sheet of paper is, because everything else is.

Suppose we try to return one of the elements to its source. Suppose we return the sunshine to the sun. Do you think that this sheet of paper will be possible? No, without sunshine nothing can be. And if we return the logger to his mother, then we have no sheet of paper either. The fact is that this sheet of paper is made up only of "non-paper elements." And if we return these non-paper elements to their sources, then there can be no paper at all. Without "non-paper elements," like mind, logger, sunshine and so on, there will be no paper. As thin as this sheet of paper is, it contains everything in the universe in it.

— *The Heart of Understanding*

ROSES AND GARBAGE

Defiled or immaculate. Dirty or pure. These are concepts we form in our mind. A beautiful rose we have just cut and placed in our vase is immaculate. It smells so good, so pure, so fresh. It supports the idea of immaculateness. The opposite is a garbage can. It smells horrible, and it is filled with rotten things.

But that is only when you look on the surface. If you look more deeply you will see that in just five or six days, the rose will become part of the garbage. You do not need to wait five days to see it. If you just look at the rose, and you look deeply, you can see it now. And if you look into the garbage can, you see that in a few months its contents can be transformed into lovely vegetables, and even a rose. If you are a good organic gardener and you have the eyes of a bodhisattva, looking at a rose you can see the garbage, and looking at the garbage you can see a rose. Roses and garbage inter-are. Without a rose, we cannot have garbage; and without garbage, we cannot have a rose. They need each other very much. The rose and garbage are equal. The garbage is just as precious as the rose. If we look deeply at the concepts of defilement and immaculateness, we return to the notion of inter-being.

In the city of Manila there are many young prostitutes, some of them only fourteen or fifteen years old. They are very unhappy young ladies. They did not want to be prostitutes. Their families are poor and these young girls went to the city to look for some kind of job, like a street vendor, to make money to send back to their families. Of course this is true not only in Manila, but in Ho Chi Minh City in Vietnam, in New York City, and in Paris also. It is true that in the city you can make money more easily than in the countryside, so we can imagine how a young girl may have been tempted to go there to help her family. But after only a few weeks there, she was persuaded by a clever person to work for her and to earn perhaps one hundred times more money. Because she was so young and did not know much about life, she accepted, and became a prostitute. Since that time, she has carried the feeling of being impure, defiled, and this causes her great suffering. When she looks at other young girls, dressed beautifully, belonging to good families, a wretched feeling wells up in her, and this feeling of defilement has become her hell.

But if she could look deeply at herself and at the whole situation, she would see that she is like this because other people are like that. "This is like this, because that is like that." So how can a so-called good girl, belonging to a good family, be proud? Because their way of life is like this, the other girl has to be like that. No one among us has clean hands. No one of us can claim it is not our responsibility. The girl in Manila is that way because of the way we are. Looking into the life of that young prostitute, we see the non-prostitute people. And looking at the non-prostitute people, and at the way we live our lives, we see the prostitute. This helps to create that, and that helps to create this.

Let us look at wealth and poverty. The affluent society and the society deprived of everything inter-are. The wealth of one society is made of the poverty of the other. "This is like this, because that is like that." Wealth is made of non-wealth elements, and poverty is made by non-poverty elements. It is exactly the same as with the sheet of paper. So we must be careful. We should not imprison ourselves in concepts. The truth is that everything is everything else. We can only inter-be, we cannot just be. And we are responsible for everything that happens around us. Only by seeing with the eyes of interbeing can that young girl be freed from her suffering.

We are not separate. We are inextricably inter-related. The rose is the garbage, and the non-prostitute is the prostitute. The rich man is the very poor woman, and the Buddhist is the non-Buddhist. The non-Buddhist cannot help but be a Buddhist, because we inter-are. The emancipation of the young prostitute will come as she sees into the nature of interbeing. She will know that she is bearing the fruit of the whole world. And if we look into ourselves and see her, we bear her pain, and the pain of the whole world.   — *The Heart of Understanding*

THE SUN MY HEART

We know that if our heart stops beating, the flow of our life will stop, and so we cherish our heart very much. Yet we do not often take the time to notice that there are other things, outside of our bodies, that are also essential for our survival. Look at the immense light we call the sun. If it stops shining, the flow of our life will also stop, and so the sun is our second heart, our heart outside of our body. This immense "heart" gives all life on Earth the warmth necessary for existence. Plants live thanks to the sun. Their leaves absorb the sun's energy, along with carbon dioxide from the air, to produce food for the tree, the flower, the plankton. And thanks to plants, we and other animals can live. All of us — people, animals, and plants — "consume" the sun, directly and indirectly. We cannot begin to describe all the effects of the sun, that great heart outside of our body. In fact, our body is not limited to what lies inside the boundary of our skin. Our body is much greater, much more immense. If the layer of air around our Earth disappears even for an instant, "our" life will end. There is no phenomenon in the universe that does not intimately concern us, from a pebble resting at the bottom of the ocean, to the movement of a galaxy millions of light years away. The poet Walt Whitman said, "I believe a leaf of grass is no less than the journey-work of the stars...." These words are not philosophy. They come from the depths of his soul. He said, "I am large, I contain multitudes."

— The Sun My Heart

THE FLOWER IS STILL BLOOMING

There is a practice called Meditation on True Emptiness, in which the practitioner lets go of habitual ways of thinking about being and non-being by realizing that these concepts were formed by incorrectly perceiving things as independent and permanent. When an apple tree produces flowers, we don't see apples yet, and so we might say, "There are flowers but no apples on this tree." We say this because we do not see the latent presence of the apples in the flowers. Time will gradually reveal the apples.

When we look at a chair, we see the wood, but we fail to observe the tree, the forest, the carpenter, or our own mind. When we meditate on it, we can see the entire universe in all its interwoven and interdependent relations in the chair. The presence of the wood reveals the presence of the tree. The presence of the leaf reveals the presence of the sun. The presence of the apple blossom reveals the presence of the apple. Meditators can see the one in the many, and the many in the one. Even before they see the chair, they can see its presence in the heart of living reality. The chair is not separate. It exists only in its interdependent relations with everything else in the universe. It *is* because all other things *are*. If it *is not,* then all other things *are not* either.

Every time we use the word "chair" or the concept "chair" forms in our mind, reality is severed in half. There is "chair" and there is everything which is "non-chair." This kind of separation is both violent and absurd. The sword of conceptualization functions this way because we do not realize that the chair is made entirely from non-chair elements. Since all non-chair elements are present in the chair, how can we separate them? An awakened individual vividly sees the non-chair elements when looking at the chair, and realizes that the chair has no boundaries, no beginning, and no end.

To deny the existence of a chair is to deny the presence of the whole universe. A chair which exists cannot become non-existent, even if we chop it up into small pieces or burn it. If we could succeed in destroying one chair, we could destroy the entire universe. The concept of "beginning and end" is closely linked with the concept of "being and non-being." For example, from what moment in time can we say that a particular bicycle has come into existence and from what moment is it no longer existent? If we say that it begins to exist the moment the last part is assembled, does that mean we cannot say, "This bicycle needs just one more part," the prior moment? And when it is broken and cannot be ridden, why do we call it "a broken bicycle"? If we meditate on the moment the bicycle is and the moment it is no longer, we will notice that the bicycle cannot be placed in the categories "being and non-being" or beginning and end."

Did the Indian poet Rabindranath Tagore exist before his birth or not? Does he exist after his death or has he ceased to exist? If you accept the principle of "interpenetration" or the principle of "interbeing," you cannot say that there has ever been a time when "Tagore *is not,*" even the times before his birth or after his death. If Tagore is not, the entire universe cannot be, nor can you or I exist. It is not because of his "birth" that Tagore exists, nor because of his "death" that he does not exist.

I have heard several friends express regret that they did not live at the time of the Buddha. I think that even if they passed him on the street, they would not recognize him. Not only Tagore and Shakyamuni Buddha, but all of us are without beginning and without end. I am here because you are there. If anyone of us does not exist, no one else can exist either. Reality cannot be confined by concepts of being, non-being, birth, and death. The term "true emptiness" can be used to describe reality and to destroy all ideas which imprison and divide us and which artificially create a reality. Without a mind free from preconceived ideas, we cannot penetrate reality. Scientists are coming to realize that they cannot use ordinary language to describe non-conceptual insights. Scientific language is beginning to have the symbolic nature of poetry. Today such words as "charm" and "color" are being used to describe properties of particles that have no conceptual counterpart in the "macro-realm." Some day reality will reveal itself beyond all conceptualizations and measurements. — *The Sun My Heart*

HAPPY CONTINUATION

What is the date on which you were born, your birth date? Before that date, did you already exist? Were you already there before you were born? Let me help you. To be born means from nothing you become something. My question is, before you were born, were you already there?

Suppose a hen is about to lay an egg. Before she gives birth, do you think the egg is already there? Yes, of course. It is inside. You also were inside before you were outside. That means that before you were born, you already existed — inside your mother. The fact is that if something is already there, it does not need to be born. To be born means from nothing you become something. If you are already something, what is the use of being born?

So, your so-called birthday is really your Continuation Day. The next time you celebrate, you can say, "Happy Continuation Day." I think that we may have a better concept of when we were born. If we go back nine months, to the time of our conception, we have a better date to put on our birth certificates. In China, and also in Vietnam, when you are born, you are already considered one year old. So we say we begin to be at the time of our conception in our mother's womb, and we write down that date on our birth certificate.

But the question remains: Before even that date did you exist or not? If you say, "Yes," I think you are correct. Before your conception you were there already, maybe half in your father, half in your mother. Because from nothing, we can never become something. Can you name one thing that was once a nothing? A cloud? Do you think that a cloud can be born out of nothing? Before becoming a cloud, it was water, maybe flowing as a river. It was not nothing. Do you agree?

We cannot conceive the birth of anything. There is only continuation. Please look back even further and you will see that you not only exist in your father and mother, but you also exist in your grandparents and in your great grandparents. As I look more deeply, I can see that in a former life I was a cloud. This is not poetry; it is science. Why do I say that in a former life I was a cloud? Because I am still a cloud. Without the cloud, I cannot be here. I am the cloud, the river, and the air at this very moment, so I know that in the past I have been a cloud, a river, and the air. And I was a rock. I was the minerals in the water. This is not a question of belief in reincarnation. This is the history of life on Earth. We have been gas, sunshine, water, fungi, and plants. We have been single-celled beings. The Buddha said that in one of his former lives, he was a tree. He was a fish. He was a deer. These are not superstitious things. Everyone of us has been a cloud, a deer, a bird, a fish, and we continue to be these things, not just in former lives.

This is not just the case with birth. Nothing can be born, and also nothing can die. Do you think that a cloud can die? To die means that from something you become nothing. Do you think that we can make something a nothing? Let us go back to our sheet of paper. We may have the illusion that to destroy it all we have to do is light a match and burn it up. But if we burn a sheet of paper, some of it will become smoke, and the smoke will rise and continue to be. The heat that is caused by the burning paper will enter into the cosmos and penetrate other things, because the heat is the next life of the paper. The ash that is formed will become part of the soil and the sheet of paper, in his or her next life, might be a cloud and a rose at the same time. We have to be very careful and attentive in order to realize that this sheet of paper has never been born, and it will never die. It can take on other forms of being, but we are not capable of transforming a sheet of paper into nothingness.

Everything is like that, even you and I. We are not subject to birth and death. A Zen master might give a student a subject of meditation like, "What was your face before your parents were born?" This is an invitation to go on a journey in order to recognize yourself. If you do well, you can see your former lives as well as your future lives. Please remember that we are not talking about philosophy; we are talking about reality. Look at your hand and ask yourself, "Since when has my hand been around?" If I look deeply into my hand I can see it has been around for a long time, more than three hundred thousand years. I see many generations of ancestors in there, not just in the past, but in the present moment, still alive. I am only the continuation. I have never died once. If I had died even once, how could my hand still be here?

The French scientist Lavoisier said, "Nothing is created, and nothing is destroyed." Even the best contemporary scientists cannot reduce something as small as a speck of dust or an electron to nothingness. One form of energy can only become another form of energy. Something can never become nothing, and this includes a speck of dust.

One autumn day, I was in a park, absorbed in the contemplation of a very small but beautiful leaf, in the shape of a heart. Its color was almost red, and it was barely hanging on the branch, nearly ready to fall down. I spent a long time with it, and I asked the leaf a lot of questions. I found out the leaf had been a mother to the tree. Usually we think that the tree is the mother and the leaves are just children, but as I looked at the leaf I saw that the leaf is also a mother to the tree. The sap that the roots take up is only water and minerals, not good enough to nourish the tree, so the tree distributes that sap to the leaves. And the leaves take the responsibility of transforming that rough sap into elaborated sap and, with the help of the sun and gas, sending it back in order to nourish the tree. Therefore, the leaves are also the mother to the tree. And since the leaf is linked to the tree by a stem, the communication between them is easy to see.

We do not have a stem linking us to our mother any more, but when we were in her womb we had a very long stem, an umbilical cord. The oxygen and the nourishment we needed came to us through that stem. Unfortunately, on the day that we call our birthday, it was cut off and we received the illusion that we are independent. That is a mistake. We continue to rely on our mother for a very long time, and we have several other mothers as well. The Earth is our Mother. We have a great many stems linking us to our Mother Earth. There is a stem linking us with the cloud. If there is no cloud, there is no water for us to drink. We are made of at least seventy percent water, and the stem between the cloud and us is really there. This is also the case with the river, the forest, the logger, and the farmer. There are hundreds of thousands of stems linking us to everything in the cosmos, and therefore we can be. Do you see the link between you and me? If you are not there, I am not here. That is certain. If you do not see it yet, look more deeply and I am sure you will see. As I said, this is not philosophy. You really have to see.

I asked the leaf whether it was scared because it was autumn and the other leaves were falling. The leaf told me, "No. During the whole spring and summer I was very alive. I worked hard and helped nourish the tree, and much of me is in the tree. Please do not say that I am just this form, because the form of leaf is only a tiny part of me. I am the whole tree. I know that I am already inside the tree, and when I go back to the soil, I will continue to nourish the tree. That's why I do not worry. As I leave this branch and float to the ground, I will wave to the tree and tell her, 'I will see you again very soon.' "

That day there was a wind blowing and, after a while, I saw the leaf leave the branch and float down to the soil, dancing joyfully, because as it floated it saw itself already there in the tree. It was so happy. I bowed my head, and I knew that we have a lot to learn from the leaf.

A wave on the ocean has a beginning and an end, a birth and a death. But the wave is empty. The wave is full of water, but it is empty of a separate self. A wave is a form which has been made possible thanks to the existence of wind and water. If a wave only sees its form, with its beginning and end, it will be afraid of birth and death. But if the wave sees that it is water, identifies itself with the water, then it will be emancipated from birth and death. Each wave is born and is going to die, but the water is free from birth and death.

When I was a child I used to play with a kaleidoscope. I took a tube and a few pieces of ground glass, turned it a little bit, and saw many wonderful sights. Every time I made a small movement with my fingers, one sight would disappear and another would appear. I did not cry at all when the first spectacle disappeared, because I knew that nothing was lost. Another beautiful sight always followed. If you are the wave and you become one with the water, looking at the world with the eyes of water, then you are not afraid of going up, going down, going up, going down. But please do not be satisfied with speculation, or take my word for it. You have to enter it, taste it, and be one with it yourself. And that can be done through meditation, not only in the meditation hall, but throughout your daily life. While you cook a meal, while you clean the house, while you go for a walk, you can look at things and try to see them in the nature of emptiness. "Emptiness" is an optimistic word; it is not at all pessimistic. I have seen people die very peacefully, with a smile, because they see that birth and death are only waves on the surface of the ocean, are just the spectacle in the kaleidoscope.

So you see there are many lessons we can learn from the cloud, the water, the wave, the leaf, and the kaleidoscope. From everything else in the cosmos, too. If you look at anything carefully, deeply enough, you discover the mystery of interbeing, and once you have seen it you will no longer be subject to fear — fear of birth, or fear of death. Birth and death are only ideas we have in our mind, and these ideas cannot be applied to reality. It is just like the idea of above and below. We are very sure that when we point our hand up, it is above, and when we point in the opposite direction, it is below. Heaven is above, and Hell is below. But the people who are sitting right now on the other side of the planet must disagree, because the idea of the above and below does not apply to the cosmos, exactly like the idea of birth and death.

So please continue to look back and you will see that you have always been here. Let us look together and penetrate into the life of a leaf, so we may be one with the leaf. Let us penetrate and be one with the cloud, or with the wave, to realize our own nature as water and be free from our fear. If we look very deeply, we will transcend birth and death.

Tomorrow, I will continue to be. But you will have to be very attentive to see me. I will be a flower, or a leaf. I will be in these forms and I will say hello to you. If you are attentive enough, you will recognize me, and you may greet me. I will be very happy.   — *The Heart of Understanding*

INTERPENETRATION

There is no phenomenon in the universe that does not intimately concern us, from a pebble resting at the bottom of the ocean, to the movement of a galaxy millions of light years away.

All phenomena are interdependent. When we think of a speck of dust, a flower, or a human being, our thinking cannot break loose from the idea of unity, of one, of calculation. We see a line drawn between one and many, one and not one. But if we truly realize the interdependent nature of the dust, the flower, and the human being, we see that unity cannot exist without diversity. Unity and diversity interpenetrate each other freely. Unity is diversity, and diversity is unity. This is the principle of interbeing.

If you are a mountain climber or someone who enjoys the countryside or the forest, you know that forests are our lungs outside of our bodies. Yet we have been acting in a way that has allowed millions of square miles of land to be deforested, and we have also destroyed the air, the rivers, and parts of the ozone layer. We are imprisoned in our small selves, thinking only of some comfortable conditions for this small self, while we destroy our large self. If we want to change the situation, we must begin by being our true selves. To be our true selves means we have to *be* the forest, the river, and the ozone layer. If we visualize ourselves as the forest, we will experience the hopes and fears of the trees. If we don't do this, the forest will die, and we will lose our chance for peace. When we understand that we inter-are with the trees, we will know that it is up to us to make an effort to keep the trees alive. In the last twenty years, our automobiles and factories have created acid rain that has destroyed so many trees. Because we inter-are with the trees, we know that if they do not live, we too will disappear very soon.

We humans think we are smart, but an orchid, for example, knows how to produce noble, symmetrical flowers, and a snail knows how to make a beautiful, well-proportioned shell. Compared with their knowledge, ours is not worth much at all. We should bow deeply before the orchid and the snail and join our palms reverently before the monarch butterfly and the magnolia tree. The feeling of respect for all species will help us recognize the noblest nature in ourselves.

An oak tree is an oak tree. That is all an oak tree needs to do. If an oak tree is less than an oak tree, we will all be in trouble. In our former lives, we were rocks, clouds, and trees. We have also been an oak tree. This is not just Buddhist; it is scientific. We humans are a young species. We were plants, we were trees, and now we have become humans. We have to remember our past existences and be humble. We can learn a lot from an oak tree.

All life is impermanent. We are all children of the Earth, and, at some time, she will take us back to herself again. We are continually rising from Mother Earth, being nurtured by her, and then returning to her. Like us, plants are born, live for a period of time, and then return to the Earth. When they decompose, they fertilize our gardens. Living vegetables and decomposing vegetables are part of the same reality. Without one, the other cannot be. After six months, compost becomes fresh vegetables again. Plants and the Earth rely on each other. Whether the Earth is fresh, beautiful, and green, or arid and parched depends on the plants.

It also depends on us. Our way of walking on the Earth has a great influence on animals and plants. We have killed so many animals and plants and destroyed their environments.

Many are now extinct. In turn, our environment is now harming us. We are like sleepwalkers, not knowing what we are doing or where we are heading. Whether we can wake up or not depends on whether we can walk mindfully on our Mother Earth. The future of all life, including our own, depends on our mindful steps.

Birds' songs express joy, beauty, and purity, and evoke in us vitality and love. So many beings in the universe love us unconditionally. The trees, the water, and the air don't ask anything of us; they just love us. Even though we need this kind of love, we continue to destroy them. By destroying the animals, the air, and the trees, we are destroying ourselves. We must learn to practice unconditional love for all beings so that the animals, the air, the trees, and the minerals can continue to be themselves.

Our ecology should be a deep ecology — not only deep, but universal. There is pollution in our consciousness. Television, films, and newspapers are forms of pollution for us and our children. They sow seeds of violence and anxiety in us and pollute our consciousness, just as we destroy our environment by farming with chemicals, clear-cutting the trees, and polluting the water. We need to protect the ecology of the Earth and the ecology of the mind, or this kind of violence and recklessness will spill over into even more areas of life.

Our Earth, our green beautiful Earth is in danger, and all of us know it. Yet we act as if our daily lives have nothing to do with the situation of the world. If the Earth were your body, you would be able to feel many areas where she is suffering. Many people are aware of the world's suffering, and their hearts are filled with compassion. They know what needs to be done, and they engage in political, social, and environmental work to try to change things. But after a period of intense involvement, they become discouraged, because they lack the strength needed to sustain a life of action. Real strength is not in power, money, or weapons, but in deep, inner peace.

If we change our daily lives — the way we think, speak, and act — we change the world. The best way to take care of the environment is to take care of the environmentalist.

— *The Sun My Heart*

PARADISE

As a novice I was required to read Buddhist philosophy. I was only sixteen and unable to grasp concepts like Interdependent Co-Arising, and Oneness of Subject and Object. It was difficult to understand why the perceiver could not exist independently from the object being perceived. I managed to get a high mark on my philosophy exams, but I didn't really understand. I reasoned that, thanks to awareness, the finite world of phenomena could partake of the transcendent realm of consciousness. Being can only be defined in opposition to non-being, and if there is no awareness of either being or non-being, it is as though nothing exists. The deeper implications were not at all clear.

As I write these lines, no one else has read them yet. These lines that contain my thoughts, feelings, paper, ink, time, space, and handwriting, as well as all the other phenomena that have contributed to their existence, exist only in my consciousness. Readers who may one day read these lines also lie within my consciousness. All phenomena — Vietnam with her flowering grapefruit and orange trees, graceful coconut trees, and towering areca palms, and the lively city of New York, with its sun, snow, clouds, moon, and stars — lie within my own consciousness. They are merely concepts. My world, including all my friends and readers, all the grapefruit and starfruit trees I have ever touched or thought about, is a world of concepts. When you read these lines, will you see me in them? This city as well as my thoughts and feelings will then become concepts in your consciousness. For you, these concepts are not the result of direct contact with the objects of my consciousness.

Void of physical reality, these concepts are shared through the medium of consciousness. The physical basis of consciousness, both personal and collective, has disappeared.

In the conceptual world, subject and object are two sides of the same coin. This became clear to me late one night less than two years ago, when I was staying at Bamboo Forest Temple. I awoke at 2:30 a.m. and could not get back to sleep. I lay quietly until I heard the first bell. Then I sat up and tried to locate my slippers with my feet, but they must have been too far beneath the bed. So I walked to the window barefoot. The cool floor beneath my feet felt totally refreshing and invigorating. I leaned against the windowsill and peered outside. It was still too dark to see anything, but I knew that the plants in the garden were still there — the oleander bush still stood in the same corner and the wildflowers still grew beneath the window. I experienced how the subject of awareness cannot exist apart from the object of awareness. The oleander and the wildflowers were the objects of consciousness. Subject and object of consciousness cannot be aware of anything. Mountains and rivers, Earth and sun, all lie within the heart of consciousness. When that realization arises, time and space dissolve. Cause and effect, birth and death, all vanish. Though we dwell a hundred thousand light years from a star, we can cross that distance in a flash. The saints of the past can return to the present in a microsecond, their presence as vivid as a bright flame.

I stood by the window and smiled. Someone seeing me grinning like that might have thought me deranged. The curtain of night was totally black, but not without meaning. This was infinitely clear in my consciousness. All of miraculous existence was illuminated by that smile.

You are there, because I am here. We inter-are. If we do not exist, nothing exists. Subject and object, host and guest, are part of each other. I knew that when morning came, I would not find anything new or unusual about the visible world. The blue sky in the west and the pink horizon in the east exist only in my consciousness. Blue does not have a separate life, nor does pink. They are only blue and pink in my consciousness. It is the same with birth and death, same and different, coming and going. These are all images in our consciousness. If you look into my eyes, you will see yourself. If you are radiant, my eyes will be radiant. If you are miraculous, my consciousness will be miraculous. If you are distant and remote, I will be distant and remote. Look into my eyes and you will know if your universe is bright or dark, infinite or finite, mortal or immortal.

As my smile flashed in the dark night, I felt as gentle as a cloud, as light as a feather floating on a stream of cool water, my head held by the little waves. Looking up, I saw the blue sky and white clouds that had passed during the day. The clouds were still white, the sky was still blue, perhaps even whiter and more blue. Is that not a sign of the birthless and deathless nature of reality? I heard the autumn leaves rustling in the forest, grasses in the fields.

Then I spotted a star in the sky and immediately returned to the place where I was standing, my feet touching the cool floor and my hands resting on the windowsill. "I am here," the star said. "Because I exist, the universe exists. Because I exist, you exist. Because I exist, the pebbles and the distant clouds exist. If all of these can't truly exist, how can I? The existence of a speck of dust makes everything else possible. If dust does not exist, neither does the universe, nor you, nor I."

I am happy to be on this Earth. The river reflects everything in herself. Thanks to the river's flow, the flux of life is possible. And death lies within life, because without death there could be no life. Let us welcome the flow. Let us welcome impermanence and non-self. Thanks to impermanence and non-self, we have the beautiful world praised by Zen poets — the sheen of banana trees, the tall and perfumed areca trees reaching to the sun. The Earth is filled with dust. Our eyes are filled with dust. There is no need to seek a Pure Land somewhere else. We only need lift our heads and see the moon and the stars. The essential quality is awareness. If we open our eyes, we will see. I am sure that heaven has areca, starfruit, lime, and grapefruit trees. I laugh when I think how I once sought paradise as a realm outside of the world of birth and death. It is right in the world of birth and death that the miraculous truth is revealed.

Vietnam has extraordinary rainstorms. One day, I sat by the window of a friend's home and watched a scene I could have watched forever. Across the street was a low-roofed dry goods store. Coils of rope and barbed wire, pots and pans hung from the eaves. Hundreds of items were on display — fish sauce and bean sauce, candles and peanut candy. The store was so packed and dimly lit, it was difficult to distinguish one object from another as the rainstorm darkened the street. A young boy, no more than five or six, wearing a simple pair of shorts, his skin darkened by hours of play in the sun, sat on a little stool on the front step of the store. He was eating a bowl of rice, protected by the overhang. Rain ran off the roof making puddles in front of where he sat. He held his rice bowl in one hand and his chopsticks in the other, and he ate slowly, his eyes riveted on the stream of water pouring from the roof. Large drops exploded into bubbles on the surface of a puddle. Though I was across the street, I could tell that his rice was mixed with pieces of duck egg and sprinkled with fish sauce. He raised his chopsticks slowly to his mouth, savoring each small mouthful. He gazed at the rain and appeared to be utterly content, the very image of well-being. I could feel his heart beating. His lungs, stomach, liver, and all his organs were working in perfect harmony. If he had had a toothache, he could not have been enjoying the effortless peace of that moment. I looked at him as one might admire a perfect jewel, a flower, or a sunrise. Truth and paradise revealed themselves. I was completely absorbed by his image. He seemed to be a divine being, a young god embodying the bliss of well-being with every glance of his eyes and every bite of rice he took. He was completely free of worry or anxiety. He had no thought of being poor. He did not compare his simple black shorts to the fancy clothes of other children. He did not feel sad because he had no shoes. He did not mind that he sat on a hard stool rather than a cushioned chair. He felt no longing. He was completely at peace in the moment. Just by watching him, the same well-being flooded my body.

A violet shadow flitted across the street. The boy looked up for an instant, his eyes startled by the blur of bright color, and then he returned his gaze to the water bubbles dancing on the puddle. He chewed his rice and egg carefully, and watched the rain in delight. He paid no more attention to the passersby, two young women dressed in red and purple *ao dai,* carrying umbrellas. Suddenly he turned his head and looked down the street. He smiled and became so absorbed in something new, I turned to look down the street myself. Two young children were pulling a third child in a wooden wagon. The three did not have a stitch of clothing on and were having a grand time splashing in the puddles. The wheels of the wagon spun round and round, spraying water whenever the wagon hit a puddle. I looked back at the boy on the doorstep. He had stopped eating to watch the other children. His eyes sparkled. I believe my eyes reflected his in that moment, and I shared his delight. Perhaps my delight was not as great as his, or perhaps it was even greater because I was so aware of being happy.

Then I heard him call out, "Coming, Mama," and he stood up and went back into the shop. I guessed his mother had called him back in to refill his rice bowl, but he did not come out again. Perhaps he was now eating with his parents, who scolded him for dawdling so long over his first bowl. If that was the case, poor child! His parents did not know he had just been in paradise. They did not know that when the mind divides reality up, when it judges and discriminates, it kills paradise. Please do not scold the sunlight. Do not chastise the clear stream, or the little birds of spring.

How can you enter paradise unless you become like a little child? You can't see reality with eyes that discriminate or base all their understanding on concepts. As I write these lines, I long to return to the innocence of childhood. I want to play the Vietnamese children's game of examining the whorls of a friend's hair — "one whorl your allegiance is with your father, two whorls with your mother, three whorls with your aunt, many whorls with your country." I'd love to make a snowball and hurl it all the way back to Vietnam.

— Fragrant Palm Leaves

ARMFULS OF POETRY, DROPS OF SUNSHINE

(This poem has a lot of interbeing in it. The sun is green, because you can recognize it in the vegetables. Poetry is born from the wood that is burning in the stove. Without it, I cannot write. The last lines of the poem speak about the work of helping hungry children. —Thich Nhat Hahn)

Sunshine rides on space and poetry on sunshine.
Poetry gives birth to sunshine, and sunshine to poetry.

Sun treasured in the heart of the bitter melon,
poetry made of steam rising from a bowl of soup in
　　Winter.
The wind is lurking outside, swirling.
Poetry is back to haunt the old hills and prairies.
Yet the poor thatched hut remains on the river shore,
　　waiting.

Spring carries poetry in its drizzle.
The fire sparkles poetry in its orange flame.

Sunshine stored in the heart of the fragrant wood,
warm smoke leading poetry back to the pages
of an unofficial history book.

Sunshine, though absent from space,
fills the now rose-colored stove.

Sunshine reaching out takes the color of smoke;
poetry in its stillness, the color of the misty air.

Spring rain holds poetry in its drops
which bend down to kiss the soil,
so that the seeds may sprout.
Following the rain, poetry comes to dwell on each leaf.
Sunshine has a green color, and poetry a pink one.
Bees deliver warmth to the flowers from the sunshine
they carry on their wings.
On sunshine footsteps to the deep forest,
poetry drinks the nectar with joy.
With the excitement of celebration,
butterflies and bees crowd the Earth.
Sunshine makes up the dance, and poetry the song.

Drops of sweat fall on the hard ground.
Poems fly along the furrows.
The hoe handily on my shoulder, poetry flows from the
    breath.
Sunshine wanes away down the river
and the silhouette of the late afternoon lingers reluctantly.
Poetry is leaving for the horizon
Where the King of Light is blanketing himself in clouds.

A green sun found in a basketful of fresh vegetables,
a tasty and well-cooked sun smells delicious in a bowl of
    rice.
Poetry looks with a child's eyes.
Poetry feels with a weather-beaten face.
Poetry stays within each attentive look.
Poetry — the hands that work the poor and arid land
    somewhere
far away.

The smiling sun brightening up the sunflower;
the ripe and full sun hiding itself in an August peach;
poetry follows each meditative step,
poetry lines up the pages.

Discreetly,
within closed food packages,
poetry nurtures love.

— *Call Me by My True Names*

3

Seeds of Compassion

Compassion is not an idea or something we can imagine. It is a mental formation that has an immediate result in action of body, speech, or mind. It is rooted in understanding. When we understand why we suffer we can be compassionate to ourselves. When we understand how others suffer then we can be compassionate to them. We think that the other is a separate self, bent on doing harm to us or to our world. However, the other is a composite, a result of numberless causes and conditions which have come together. We only need to understand those causes and conditions and we shall understand the actions and the person of the other. Because this is, that is. When some persons cause me to suffer, Thây has told me, I should ask if I myself, in fact, may be one of the causes and conditions which makes them what they are.

Thây knows what it is to feel angry, and he recognizes that this is a very human emotion. The task is not to eradicate anger but to transform it. When Thây heard that an American military man had said that they had to destroy the town of Ben Tre in order to save it, he was very angry, and he had to practice hard to embrace his anger with compassion by means of conscious breathing. In 1986 Thây encouraged us to write a small poem of four lines to use as soon as we feel ourselves becoming angry so that we remember not to do or say something that we shall later regret.

Thây himself composed a couple of short poems. One of them is
as follows:

> Feeling angry in the historical dimension,
> I close my eyes and look deeply.
> Three hundred years from now,
> Where will you be? Where shall I be?

— Sister Annabel Laity

PLEASE CALL ME BY MY TRUE NAMES

(This poem was written in 1978, during the time of helping the
boat people. — Thich Nhat Hanh)

> Don't say that I will depart tomorrow —
> even today I am still arriving.
> Look deeply: every second I am arriving
> to be a bud on a Spring branch,
> to be a tiny bird, with still-fragile wings,
> learning to sing in my new nest,
> to be caterpillar in the heart of a flower,
> to be a jewel hiding itself in a stone.
>
> I still arrive, in order to laugh and to cry,
> to fear and to hope.
> The rhythm of my heart is the birth and death
> of all that is alive.
>
> I am a mayfly metamorphosing
> on the surface of the river.
> And I am the bird
> that swoops down to swallow the mayfly.
>
> I am a frog swimming happily
> in the clear water of a pond.

And I am the grass-snake
that silently feeds itself on the frog.

I am the child in Uganda, all skin and bones,
my legs as thin as bamboo sticks.
And I am the arms merchant,
selling deadly weapons to Uganda.

I am the twelve-year-old girl,
refugee on the small boat,
who throws herself into the ocean
after being raped by a sea pirate.
And I am the pirate,
my heart not yet capable
of seeing and loving.

I am a member of the politburo,
with plenty of power in my hands.
And I am the man who has to pay
his "debt of blood" to my people
dying slowly in a forced-labor camp.

My joy is like Spring, so warm
it makes flowers bloom all over the Earth.
My pain is like a river of tears,
so vast it fills the four oceans.

Please call me by my true names,
so I can hear all my cries and laughter at once,
so I can see that my joy and pain are one.

Please call me by my true names,
so I can wake up
and the door of my heart
could be left open,
the door of compassion.

      — *Call Me by My True Names*

TRANSFORMING OUR COMPOST

When we look deeply into ourselves, we see both flowers and garbage. Each of us has anger, hatred, depression, racial discrimination, and many other kinds of garbage in us, but there is no need for us to be afraid. In the way that a gardener knows how to transform compost into flowers, we can learn the art of transforming anger, depression, and racial discrimination into love and understanding. This is the work of meditation.

According to Buddhist psychology, our consciousness is divided into two parts, like a house with two floors. On the ground floor there is a living room, and we call this "mind consciousness." Below the ground level, there is a basement, and we call this "store consciousness." In the store consciousness, everything we have ever done, experienced, or perceived is stored in the form of a seed, or a film. Our basement is an archive of every imaginable kind of film stored on a videocassette. Upstairs in the living room, we sit in a chair and watch these films as they are brought up from the basement.

Certain movies, such as *Anger, Fear,* or *Despair,* seem to have the ability to come up from the basement all by themselves. They open the door to the living room and pop themselves into our videocassette recorder whether we choose them or not. When that happens, we feel stuck, and we have no choice but to watch them. Fortunately, each film has a limited length, and when it is over, it returns to the basement. But each time it is viewed by us, it establishes a better position on the archive shelf, and we know it will return soon. Sometimes a stimulus from outside, like someone saying something that hurts our feelings, triggers the showing of a film on our TV screen. We spend so much of our time watching these films, and many of them are destroying us. Learning how to stop them is important for our well-being.

Traditional texts describe consciousness as a field, a plot of land where every kind of seed can be planted — seeds of suffering, happiness, joy, sorrow, fear, anger, and hope. Store consciousness is also described as a storehouse filled with all our seeds. When a seed manifests in our mind consciousness, it always returns to the storehouse stronger. The quality of our life depends on the quality of the seeds in our store consciousness.

We may be in the habit of manifesting seeds of anger, sorrow, and fear in our mind consciousness; seeds of joy, happiness, and peace may not sprout up much. To practice mindfulness means to recognize each seed as it comes up from the storehouse and to practice watering the most wholesome seeds whenever possible, to help them grow stronger. During each moment that we are aware of something peaceful and beautiful, we water seeds of peace and beauty in us, and beautiful flowers bloom in our consciousness. The length of time we water a seed determines the strength of that seed. For example, if we stand in front of a tree, breathe consciously, and enjoy it for five minutes, seeds of happiness will be watered in us for five minutes, and those seeds will grow stronger. During the same five minutes other seeds, like fear and pain, will not be watered. We have to practice this way every day. Any seed that manifests in our mind consciousness always returns to our store consciousness stronger. If we water our wholesome seeds carefully, we can trust that our store consciousness will do the work of healing.

Healing has many avenues. When we feel anger, distress, or despair, we only need to breathe in and out consciously and we recognize the feeling of anger, distress, or despair, and then we can leave the work of healing to our consciousness. But it is not only by touching our pain that we can heal. In fact, if we are not ready to do that, touching it may only make it worse. We have to strengthen ourselves first, and the easiest way to do this is by touching joy and peace. There are many wonderful things, but because we have focused our attention on what is wrong, we have not been able to touch what is *not* wrong. If we make some effort to breathe in and out and touch what is not wrong, the healing will be easier. Many of us have so much pain that it is difficult for us to touch a flower or hold the hand of a child. But we must make some effort so that we can develop the habit of touching what is beautiful and wholesome. This is the way we can assist our store consciousness to do the work of healing. If we touch what is peaceful and healing in us and around us, we help our store consciousness do the work of transformation. We let ourselves be healed by the trees, the birds, and the beautiful children. Otherwise, we will only repeat our suffering.

One wonderful seed in our store consciousness — the seed of mindfulness — when manifested, has the capacity of being aware of what is happening in the present moment. If we take one peaceful, happy step and we know that we are taking a peaceful, happy step, mindfulness is present. Mindfulness is an important agent for our transformation and healing, but our seed of mindfulness has been buried under many layers of forgetfulness and pain for a long time. We are rarely aware that we have eyes that see clearly, a heart and a liver that function well, and a non-toothache. We live in forgetfulness, looking for happiness somewhere else, ignoring and crushing the precious elements of happiness that are already in us and around us. If we breathe in and out and see that the tree is there, alive and beautiful, the seed of our mindfulness will be watered, and it will grow stronger. When we first start to practice, our mindfulness will be weak, like a fifteen-watt light bulb. But as soon as we pay attention to our breathing, it begins to grow stronger, and after practicing like that for a few weeks, it becomes as bright as a one-hundred-watt bulb. With the light of mindfulness shining, we touch many wonderful elements within and around us, and while doing so, we water the seeds of peace, joy, and happiness in us, and at the same time, we refrain from watering the seeds of unhappiness.

For us to be happy, we need to water the seed of mindfulness that is in us. Mindfulness is the seed of enlightenment, awareness, understanding, care, compassion, liberation, transformation, and healing. If we practice mindfulness, we get in touch with the refreshing and joyful aspects of life in us and around us, the things we are not able to touch when we live in forgetfulness. Mindfulness makes things like our eyes, our heart, our non-toothache, the beautiful moon, and the trees deeper and more beautiful. If we touch these wonderful things with mindfulness, they will reveal their full splendor. When we touch our pain with mindfulness, we will begin to transform it. When a baby is crying in the living room, his mother goes in right away to hold him tenderly in her arms. Because mother is made of love and tenderness, when she does that, love and tenderness penetrate the baby and, in only a few minutes, the baby will probably stop crying. Mindfulness is the mother who cares for your pain every time it begins to cry.

If you embrace a minor pain with mindfulness, it will be transformed in a few minutes. Just breathe in and out, and smile at it. But when you have a block of pain that is stronger, more time is needed. Practice sitting and walking meditation while you embrace your pain in mindfulness, and sooner or later, it will be transformed. If you have increased the quality of your mindfulness through the practice, the transformation will be quicker. When mindfulness embraces pain, it begins to penetrate and transform it, like sunshine penetrating a flower bud and helping it blossom. When mindfulness touches something beautiful, it reveals its beauty. When it touches something painful, it transforms and heals it.

The seeds of suffering are always trying to emerge. If we try to suppress them, we create a lack of circulation in our psyche and we feel sick. Practicing mindfulness helps us get strong enough to open the door to our living room and let the pain come up. Every time our pain is immersed in mindfulness, it will lose some of its strength, and later, when it returns to the store consciousness, it will be weaker. When it comes up again, if our mindfulness is there to welcome it like a mother greeting her baby, the pain will be lessened and will go back down to the basement even weaker. In this way, we create good circulation in our psyche, and we begin to feel much better. If the blood is circulating well in our body, we experience well-being. If the energy of our mental formations is circulating well between our store consciousness and mind consciousness, we also have the feeling of well-being. We do not need to be afraid of our pain if our mindfulness is there to embrace it and transform it.

Our consciousness is the totality of our seeds, the totality of our films. If the good seeds are strong, we will have more happiness. Meditation helps the seed of mindfulness grow and develop as the light within us. If we practice mindful living, we will know how to water the seeds of joy and transform the seeds of sorrow and suffering so that understanding, compassion, and loving-kindness will flower in us.   — *Touching Peace*

RELEASING OUR COWS

A lot of joy and happiness comes from getting away or leaving something behind. Suppose you are suffering from the noise, pollution, and stresses of the city. It is Friday afternoon, and you want to get away. You get in your car and drive away. Once you're in the countryside with the beautiful trees, the blue sky, and the bird song, you feel joy. The joy you experience from being in the countryside is born from having abandoned the city, from leaving something behind.

There are many things we are unable to leave behind us, which trap us. Practice looking deeply into these things. In the beginning, you may think that they are vital to your happiness, but they may actually be obstacles to your true happiness, causing you to suffer. If you are not able to be happy because you are caught by them, leaving them behind will be a source of joy for you....

One day the Buddha was sitting with a group of monks in the woods near the city of Sravasti. They had just finished a mindful lunch and were engaged in a small Dharma discussion.

Suddenly a farmer came by. He was visibly upset and shouted, "Monks! Have you seen my cows?"

The Buddha said, "No, we have not seen any cows."

"You know, monks," the man said, "I am the most miserable person on Earth. For some reason, my twelve cows all ran away this morning. I have only two acres of sesame seed plants and this year the insects ate them all. I think I am going to kill myself." The farmer was really suffering.

Out of compassion, the Buddha said, "No, sir, we have not seen your cows. Maybe you should look for them elsewhere."

When the farmer was gone, the Buddha turned to his monks, looked at them deeply, smiled, and said, "Dear friends, do you know that you are the happiest people on Earth? You don't have any cows to lose."

So, my friends, if you have cows, look deeply into the nature of your cows to see whether they have been bringing you happiness or suffering. You should learn the art of releasing your cows. The key thing is to let go and free yourself. . . .

There is a poem that describes the Buddha in this way: "The Buddha is like a full moon sailing across the empty sky." The Buddha had a lot of space around him because he did not possess anything. He didn't have any cows. That is why his happiness was immense. . . .

•

There is nothing more precious than our peace, stability, and freedom. We cannot exchange these for anything else. "Release" means we have become ourselves. We are capable of releasing all of our cows and our ideas — even our ideas of happiness. Each of us is caught in an idea of happiness. We believe that we will be truly happy when certain conditions are fulfilled. We don't realize that this idea is an obstacle to our true happiness. If we can release our idea of happiness, true happiness is born in us right away. I know some young people who think that they can only be happy if they earn a degree, get a certain job, or marry a certain person. We set up conditions for our happiness and become trapped. Happiness can come to us at any time if we are free. Why do we commit ourselves to only one idea of happiness? When we do this, we limit our happiness. If we let go of that idea, happiness will come to us from every direction.

A whole country may be under the spell of an idea of happiness for many years. A whole nation may think that unless it carries out a certain five-year program, or embraces and realizes a particular ideology, there will be no future for its citizens. Unless the nation realizes that this idea is an obstacle to its happiness, it might experience tragedy. If we are lucky, we can release such false ideas. "Breathing in, I smile. Breathing out, I release."   — *The Path of Emancipation*

REALIZING ULTIMATE REALITY

We come to the practice of meditation seeking relief from our suffering, and meditation can teach us how to transform our suffering and obtain basic relief. But the deepest kind of relief is the realization of nirvana. There are two dimensions to life, and we should be able to touch both. One is like a wave, and we call it the historical dimension. The other is like the water, and we call it the ultimate dimension, or nirvana. We usually touch just the wave, but when we discover how to touch the water, we receive the highest fruit that meditation can offer.

In the historical dimension, we have birth certificates and death certificates. The day your mother passes away, you suffer. If someone sits close to you and shows her concern, you feel some relief. You have her friendship, her support, her warm hand to hold. This is the world of waves. It is characterized by birth and death, ups and downs, being and non-being. A wave has its beginning and an end, but we cannot ascribe these characteristics to water. In the world of water, there is no birth or death, no being or non-being, no beginning or end. When we touch the water, we touch reality in its ultimate dimension and are liberated from all of those concepts.

The second-century philosopher Nagarjuna asked, "Before something was born, did it exist or not?" Before the egg was born from a chicken, was it existent or non-existent? If it were already there, how could it have been born? Since a baby is also already present in the womb of her mother, how can we say she is not yet born? Nagarjuna says that something already present cannot be born. To be born means from nothing you become something; from no one you become someone. But nothing can be born from nothing. A flower is born from soil, minerals, seeds, sunshine, rain, and many other things. Meditation reveals to us the no-birth of all things. Life is a continuation. Instead of singing "Happy Birthday," we can sing "Happy Continuation." Even the day of our mother's death is a day of continuation; she continues in many other forms.

One day as I was about to step on a dry leaf, I saw the leaf in the ultimate dimension. I saw that it was not really dead, but it was merging with the moist soil and preparing to appear on the tree the following spring in another form. I smiled at the leaf and said, "You are pretending."

Everything is pretending to be born and pretending to die, including the leaf I almost stepped on. The Buddha said, "When conditions are sufficient, the body reveals itself, and we say the body is. When conditions are not sufficient, the body cannot be perceived by us, and we say the body is not." The day of our so-called death is a day of our continuation in many other forms. If you know how to touch your mother in the ultimate dimension, she will always be there with you. If you touch your hand, your face, or your hair, and look very deeply, you can see that she is there in you, smiling. This is a deep practice, and it is also the deepest kind of relief.

Nirvana means extinction, the extinction of all notions and concepts, including the concepts of birth, death, being, non-being, coming, and going. Nirvana is the ultimate dimension of life, a state of coolness, peace, and joy. It is not a state to be attained after you die. You can touch nirvana right now by breathing, walking, and drinking your tea in mindfulness. You have been "nirvanized" since the very non-beginning. Everything and everyone is dwelling in nirvana.

Nikos Kazantzakis tells the story of St. Francis of Assisi standing in front of an almond tree in mid-winter. St. Francis asked the tree to tell him about God, and suddenly the tree began to blossom. In just a few seconds, the almond tree was covered with beautiful flowers. When I read this story, I was very impressed. I saw that St. Francis stood on the side of the ultimate dimension. It was winter; there were no leaves, flowers, or fruits, but he saw the flowers.

We may feel that we are incapable of touching the ultimate dimension, but that is not correct. We have done so already. The problem is how to do it more deeply and more frequently. The phrase, "Think globally," for example, is in the direction of touching the ultimate dimension. When we see things globally, we have more wisdom and we feel much better. We are not caught by small situations. When we see globally we avoid many mistakes, and we have a more profound view of happiness and life.

When we dwell in the historical dimension, we are tossed about by many waves. Perhaps we have a difficult time at work. Or we have to wait too long in line at the supermarket. Or we have a bad telephone connection with our friend. We feel tired, a little depressed, or angry. This is because we are caught in the present situation. But if we close our eyes and visualize the world one hundred years from now, we will see that these problems are not important. Embracing just one hundred years, we see things very differently. Imagine how drastic a change is brought about by touching the ultimate dimension!

We are entirely capable of touching the ultimate dimension. As I write this page, I am aware that my feet are on the ground in Plum Village, standing on French soil. I am also aware that France is linked to Germany, Spain, Czechoslovakia, and Russia, and even to India, China, and Vietnam. Thinking globally, I see that I am standing on more than just a spot, because when I touch Plum Village, I touch all of Europe and Asia. China is just an extension of the small piece of land under my feet. Standing on one part of the Eurasian continent, I am standing on the whole continent.

This kind of awareness transforms the spot you are standing on to include the whole Earth. When you practice walking meditation and realize that you are making steps on the beautiful planet Earth, you will see yourself and your walking quite differently, and you will be liberated from narrow views or boundaries. Each step you take, you see that you are touching the whole Earth. When you touch with that awareness, you liberate yourself from many afflictions and wrong views.

When you touch one thing with deep awareness, you touch everything. The same is true of time. When you touch one moment with deep awareness, you touch all moments. If you live one moment deeply, that moment contains all the past and all the future in it. "The one contains the all." Touching the present moment does not mean getting rid of the past or the future. As you touch the present moment, you realize that the present is made of the past and is creating the future. Touching the present, you touch the past and the future at the same time. You touch globally the infinity of time, the ultimate dimension of reality. When you drink a cup of tea very deeply, you touch the present moment and you touch the whole of time. It is what St. Francis did when he touched the almond tree so profoundly that he could see it flowering even in the middle of winter. He transcended time.

Meditation is to live each moment of life deeply. Through meditation, we see that waves are made only of water, that the historical and the ultimate dimensions are one. Even while living in the world of waves, we touch the water, knowing that a wave is nothing but water. We suffer if we touch only the waves. But if we learn how to stay in touch with the water, we feel a great relief. Touching nirvana frees us from many worries. Things that upset us in the past are not that important, even one day later—imagine when we are able to touch infinite time and space.

We come to the practice seeking relief in the historical dimension. We calm our body and mind, and establish our stillness, our freshness, and our solidity. We practice loving-kindness, concentration, and transforming our anger, and we feel some relief. But when we touch the ultimate dimension of reality, we get the deepest kind of relief. Each of us has the capacity to touch nirvana and be free from birth and death, one and many, coming and going.   —*Touching Peace*

FEELINGS AND PERCEPTIONS

Every day we have many feelings. Sometimes we are happy, sometimes we are sorrowful, sometimes angry, irritated, or afraid; and these feelings fill our mind and heart. One feeling lasts for a while, and then another comes, and another, as if there is a stream of feelings for us to deal with. Practicing meditation is to be aware of each feeling.

The Abhidharma writings of Buddhist psychology say that feelings are of three kinds: pleasant, unpleasant, and neutral. When we step on a thorn, we have an unpleasant feeling. When someone says something nice to us, "You are very smart," or "You are very beautiful," we have a pleasant feeling. And there are neutral feelings, such as when you sit there and don't feel either pleasant or unpleasant. But I have read the Abhidharma and have practiced Buddhism, and I find this analysis not correct. A so-called neutral feeling can become very pleasant. If you sit down, very beautifully, and practice breathing and smiling, you can be very happy. When you sit in this way, aware that you have a feeling of well-being, that you don't have a toothache, that your eyes are capable of seeing forms and colors, isn't it wonderful?

For some people, working is unpleasant, and they suffer when they have to work. For other people, if they are forbidden from working, it is unpleasant. I do many kinds of work, and if you forbid me from binding books, from gardening, from writing poetry, from practicing walking meditation, from teaching children, I will be very unhappy. To me, work is pleasant. Pleasant or unpleasant depends on our way of looking.

We call seeing a neutral feeling. Yet someone who has lost her sight would give anything to be able to see, and if suddenly she could, she would consider it a miraculous gift. We who have eyes capable of seeing many forms and colors are often unhappy. If we want to practice, we can go out and look at leaves, flowers, children, and clouds, and be happy. Whether or not we are happy depends on our awareness. When you have a toothache, you think that not having toothache will make you very happy. But when you don't have a toothache, often you are still not happy. If you practice awareness, you suddenly become very rich, very happy. Practicing Buddhism is a clever way to enjoy life. Happiness is available. Please help yourself to it. All of us have the capacity of transforming neutral feelings into pleasant feelings, very pleasant feelings that can last a long time. This is what we practice during sitting and walking meditation. If you are happy, all of us will profit from it. Society will profit from it. All living beings will profit from it.

On the wooden board outside of the meditation hall in Zen monasteries, there is a four-line inscription. The last line is, "Don't waste your life." Our lives are made of days and hours, and each hour is precious. Have we wasted our hours and our days? Are we wasting our lives? These are important questions. Practicing Buddhism is to be alive in each moment. When we practice sitting or walking, we have the means to do it perfectly. During the rest of the day, we also practice. It is more difficult, but it is possible. The sitting and the walking must be extended to the non-walking, non-sitting moments of our day. That is the basic principle of meditation.

Perceiving includes our ideas or concepts about reality. When you look at a pencil, you perceive it, but the pencil itself may be different from the pencil in your mind. If you look at me, the me in myself may be different from the me you perceive. In order to have a correct perception, we need to have a direct encounter.

When you look at the night sky, you might see a very beautiful star, and smile at it. But a scientist may tell you that the star is no longer there, that it was extinct ten million years ago. So our perception is not correct. When we see a very beautiful sunset, we are very happy, perceiving that the sun is there with us. In fact it was already behind the mountain eight minutes ago. It takes eight minutes for the sunshine to reach our planet. The hard fact is that we never see the sun in the present, we only see the sun of the past. Suppose while walking in the twilight, you see a snake, and you scream, but when you shine your flashlight on it, it turns out to be a rope. This is an error of perception. During our daily lives we have many misperceptions. If I don't understand you, I may be angry at you all the time. We are not capable of understanding each other, and that is the main source of human suffering.

A man was rowing his boat upstream on a very misty morning. Suddenly, he saw another boat coming downstream, not trying to avoid him. It was coming straight at him. He shouted, "Be careful! Be careful!" but the boat came right into him, and his boat was almost sunk. The man became very angry, and began to shout at the other person, to give him a piece of his mind. But when he looked closely, he saw that there was no one in the other boat. It turned out that the boat just got loose and went downstream. All his anger vanished, and he laughed and laughed. If our perceptions are not correct, they may give us a lot of bad feelings. Buddhism teaches us how to look at things deeply in order to understand their own true nature, so that we will not be misled into suffering and bad feelings.

The Buddha taught that this is like this, because that is like that. You see? Because you smile, I am happy. This is like this, therefore that is like that. And that is like that because this is like this. This is called dependent co-arising.

Suppose you and I are friends. (In fact, I hope we are friends.) My well-being, my happiness depends very much on you, and your well-being, your happiness, depends upon me. I am responsible for you, and you are responsible for me. Anything I do wrong, you will suffer, and anything you do wrong, I have to suffer. Therefore, in order to take care of you, I have to take care of myself.

The Buddha had a very special way to help us understand the object of our perception. He said that in order to understand you have to be one with what you want to understand. This is a way that is practiceable. Many years ago, I used to help a committee for orphans, victims of the war in Vietnam. From Vietnam, they sent out applications, one sheet of paper with a small picture of a child in the corner, telling the name, the age, and the conditions of the orphan. We were supposed to translate it from Vietnamese into French, English, Dutch, or German, in order to seek a sponsor, so that the child would have food to eat and books for school, and be put into the family of an aunt or an uncle or a grandparent. Then the committee could send the money to the family member to help take care of the child.

Each day I helped translate about thirty applications into French. The way I did it was to look at the picture of the child. I did not read the application; I just took time to look at the picture of the child. Usually after only thirty or forty seconds, I became one with the child. I don't know how or why, but it's always like that. Then I would pick up the pen and translate the words from the application onto another sheet. Afterwards I realized that it was not me who had translated the application; it was the child and me, who had become one. Looking at his face or her face I got motivated and I became him and he became me, and together we did the translation. It is very natural.

You don't have to practice a lot of meditation to be able to do that. You just look, you allow yourself to be, and then you lose yourself in the child, and the child in you. This is one example which illustrates the way of perception recommended by Buddha. In order to understand something, you have to be one with that something.   — *Being Peace*

TRANSFORMING ANGER

Mindfulness is like a lamp illuminating ourselves. As soon as the lamp is brought into the room, the room changes. When the sun rises the light of the sun only has to shine onto the plants for them to change, grow, and develop. The light of the sun appears not to be doing anything at all, but in truth it is doing a lot. Under the influence of the sun, the plants produce chlorophyll and become green. It is thanks to the growth of plants that the animal species have what they need to survive. If the sun keeps shining on the bud, the flower will open. When the light of the sun penetrates the flower bud, the photons transform it, and the flower opens. Our mindfulness has the same function as the light of the sun. If we shine the light of full awareness steadily on our state of mind, that state of mind will transform into something better.

Thanks to the illuminating light of awareness we can see the roots of our anger. The point of meditation is to look deeply into things in order to be able to see their nature. The nature of things is interdependent origination, the true source of everything that is. If we look into our anger, we can see its roots, such as misunderstanding (or ignorance), clumsiness (or lack of skill), the surrounding society, hidden resentment, habit (or our conditioning). These roots can be present both in ourselves and in the person who played the principal role in allowing the anger to arise. We observe mindfully in order to be able to see and to understand. Seeing and understanding are the elements of liberation which allow us to be free of the suffering which always accompanies anger. Seeing and understanding bring about love and compassion. They are the drops of balm of the bodhisattva's compassion, which cool our hearts and mind. As we have already seen, our anger is a field of energy. Thanks to our mindful observation and insight into its roots, we can change this energy into the energy of love and compassion — a constructive and healing energy.

Usually when people are angry, they say and do things which cause damage to others and themselves. There are people who speak and act in ways which wound others. They believe that doing so will release the field of angry energy which is burning in their hearts. They shout and scream, beat things, and shoot poisoned arrows of speech at others. These methods of release are dangerous.

Sometimes people try to find ways to express their anger in a less dangerous way. They may go into their room, close the door behind them, and pound a pillow with all their might. Naturally, if you beat a pillow until your energy is exhausted, your anger will subside, and you will probably experience a temporary feeling of relief — exhaustion is easier to bear than anger — but the roots of the anger remain untouched, and when the conditions are right, the same anger will arise again. Therefore, the method of mindful observation in order to see and to understand the roots of our anger is the only method that has lasting effectiveness.

As we have seen already, when anger arises, we first need to come back to our conscious breathing and sponsor our anger with mindfulness. We concentrate on our breathing in order to maintain mindfulness. We avoid listening to or looking at the person whom we regard as the cause of our anger. Usually when we are angry, we do not return to ourselves and take care of healing our anger. We want to think about the hateful aspects of the person who has made us angry — rudeness, dishonesty, cruelty, maliciousness, and so on. The more we think of them, listen to them, or look at them, the more our anger flares up. Their hatefulness may be real, imaginary, or exaggerated, but whatever it is that is making us angry, we are inclined to give our full attention to that. In fact, the root of our problem is the anger inside of us, and we have to come back to it and take care of it first of all. Like a fireman, we must put water on the blaze immediately and not waste time looking for the person who set the house on fire. "Breathing in, I know that I am angry. Breathing out, I know that I must take care of my anger." So it is better not to listen to, look at, or think about the other person, or say or do anything as long as anger persists. If we put our mind into the work of observing and calming our anger, we will avoid creating damage we will probably regret later. We may like to go outside and practice walking meditation. The fresh air, green trees, and the plants will help us greatly.

Mindfulness embraces the feeling as a mother holds her crying child in her arms and transmits her affection and care. If a mother puts all her heart and mind into caring for her baby, the baby will feel the mother's gentleness and will calm down. In the same way, we can calm the functioning of our mind.

In order to lessen the unpleasant feeling brought about by the anger, we give our whole heart and mind to the practice of walking meditation, combining our breath with our steps and giving full attention to the contact between the soles of our feet and the earth. After a while, our anger will calm down, and we become stronger. Then we can begin to observe the anger and its true nature.

We know that we cannot eat potatoes without cooking them first. We fill our pot with water, put the lid on, and light the fire. The lid of the pot, which keeps the heat inside, is the power of concentration — not to speak, not to listen, not to do anything at all, but just to concentrate our whole mind on our breathing. As soon as the pot is on the fire, the water begins to get warm. When we practice conscious breathing, although our anger is still there, it is accompanied by mindfulness, the fire under the potatoes. The anger — the potatoes — has started to transform. Half an hour later, the potatoes are cooked, and our anger is transformed. We can smile, and we know that we understand the roots of our anger, and we can face the person who precipitated it.

Our anger is rooted in our lack of understanding of ourselves and of the causes, deep-seated as well as immediate, which have brought about this unpleasant state of affairs. Anger is also rooted in desire, pride, agitation, and suspiciousness. Our method of dealing with events as they arise reflects our state of understanding as well as our state of confusion. The chief roots of our anger are in ourselves. Our environment and other people are only secondary roots.

We can put up with the damage brought about by an earthquake or a flood, but if the same damage has been caused by people, we might not show much patience, and anger and hatred may arise in us. But if we know that earthquakes and floods have causes, we should also be able to see that there are causes — deep-seated or immediate — of the harm done to us by people. We need to see and understand these causes also. We have to see hardships brought about by others as a sort of natural disaster. These people make our lives difficult because they are ignorant, prisoners of their desires or their hatreds. If we speak angrily to them and treat them as our enemy, then we are just doing what they are doing, and we are no different from them. In order to realize the state of no anger in our conscious and subconscious mind, we have to practice the meditations on love and compassion. — *Transformation and Healing*

THE MIND OF COMPASSION

The essence of love and compassion is understanding, the ability to recognize the suffering of others. We have to be in touch with the physical, material, and psychological suffering of others. To do so, we have to put ourselves "inside the skin" of the other. We must "go inside" their body, feelings, and mental formations, and experience their suffering. A shallow observation as an observer will not help us to see their suffering.

When we are in contact with the suffering of another, a feeling of compassion is born in us immediately. Compassion literally means "to suffer with" the other. Looking in order to see the suffering in another person is the work of meditation. If we sit cross-legged, follow our breathing, and observe someone mindfully, we can be in contact with his or her suffering, and the energy of compassion arises in us. We can also do this while walking, standing, lying down, sitting, speaking, and acting, not just when we are sitting in meditation. The physical and psychological suffering of that person will be clear to us in the light of our mindful observation.

When the mind of compassion arises, we have to find ways to nourish and express it. When we come into contact with the other person, our thoughts and actions should express our mind of compassion, even if that person says and does things that are not easy to accept. We practice in this way until we see clearly that our love is not contingent upon the other person apologizing or being lovable. Then we can be sure that our mind of compassion is firm and authentic.

We can begin our meditation on compassion with someone who is undergoing suffering of a physical or material kind — someone who is weak and ill, poor or oppressed, or has no protection. This kind of suffering is easy to see. We observe it deeply, either during sitting meditation or when we are actually in contact with it. We must have enough time if we are going to be in deep contact with the suffering of that person. We have to observe until the mind of compassion arises, and the substance of the mind of compassion penetrates into our being. Then the mind of compassion will envelop the object of our observation. If we observe deeply in this way, the mind of compassion will naturally be transformed into action. We will not just say, "I love her very much," but instead, "I must do something so that she will suffer less." The mind of compassion is truly present when it has the capacity of removing suffering.

After that, we can practice being in contact with more subtle forms of suffering. Sometimes the other person does not seem to be suffering at all, but we may notice that she has sorrows which have left their marks in hidden ways. Someone with more than enough material comforts can also be subject to suffering, and may even commit suicide. There are very few people who are not suffering to a greater or lesser degree. The person who has made us suffer is undoubtedly suffering too. We only need to sit down, follow our breathing, and look deeply, and naturally we will see her suffering.

We may be able to see how her misery has come about because of the lack of skill of the parents who raised her. But her parents may have been the victims of their parents. The suffering has been transmitted from generation to generation, and it has been reborn in her. If we can see that, we will no longer blame her for making us suffer. Because we understand the way in which she is also a victim. To look deeply is to understand. Once we understand, it is easy to embrace the other person in our mind of compassion.

To look deeply into the suffering of those who have caused us to suffer is a miraculous gift. Thanks to our observation, we now know that the person is suffering. He may think that his suffering will be lessened if he can cause us to suffer. Once we are in touch with his suffering, our enmity and bitterness towards him will vanish, and we will long for him to suffer less. The spring water of the compassionate mind begins to flow, and we ourselves are the first to be cleansed by it. We feel cool and light, and we can smile. We do not need two people to bring about reconciliation. When we look deeply, we become reconciled with ourselves and, for us, the problem no longer exists. Sooner or later, the other will see our attitude and share in the freshness of the stream of love which is flowing naturally in our heart.

When we reduce the suffering in others, we also bring them happiness at the same time. Although life is suffering, it also has many wonderful things like the early morning sky, the harvest moon, the forsythia bush, the violet bamboo, the stream of clear water, and the beautiful child. When we pay attention only to our suffering, we are not able to make contact with these wonderful things, and anything we say or do will not untie the knot of suffering and bring about the conditions for living joyfully. Mindful observation is the element which nourishes the tree of understanding, and compassion and love are the most beautiful flowers. When we realize the mind of love, we have to go to the one who has been the object of our mindful observation, so that our mind of love is not just an object of our imagination but is a source of energy that has an effect in the real world.

Many people think that if they do not have influence and money, they cannot realize love and compassion. In fact, the source of love and compassion is in us, and we can help many people suffer less and realize a lot of happiness without being rich or influential. One word, one action, or one thought can reduce another person's suffering and bring him joy. One word can give comfort and confidence, destroy doubt, help someone avoid a mistake, reconcile a conflict, open the door to liberation, or show him the way to success and happiness. One action can save a person's life, or help him take advantage of a rare opportunity. One thought can do the same, because thoughts lead to words and action. If love and compassion are in our hearts, every thought, word, and deed can bring about a miracle. Because understanding is the very foundation of love and compassion, the words and actions engendered by love and compassion will be ones that are helpful. When we want to help, we know how to avoid the kind of love that does more harm than good. We must always remember that love is none other than understanding.

— Transformation and Healing

LOVE MEDITATION

Mindfulness illuminates what we are doing — how we stand and sit, how we look at others, how we smile, and how we frown. With the light of mindfulness present, we recognize which actions are beneficial and which are harmful. Actions that benefit us benefit others. Actions that harm us also harm others. That is why we begin this exercise by saying, "May I learn to look at myself with the eyes of understanding and compassion." Once you have used the key of understanding to open the door of love, you will experience acceptance for yourself and others. If you cannot accept others, it is because you do not yet accept yourself.

"May I be able to recognize and touch the seeds of joy and happiness in myself" is an important practice. Our mind is described as the soil containing many seeds, positive and negative. We have to be aware of all of them. When we are in touch with our suffering, we have to know that there are other seeds, too. Our ancestors transmitted seeds of suffering to us, but also seeds of peace, freedom, joy, and happiness. Even if these seeds are buried deep in our consciousness, we can water them and help them grow stronger. Touching the seeds of joy, peace, freedom, solidity, and love within ourselves is an important practice, and we ask our friends to do the same for us. If we love someone, we have to recognize and touch the positive seeds in him every day, and refrain from watering the seeds of anger, despair, and hatred. That will help him grow in the direction of health and happiness.

When our practice has become solid and we are able to understand, love, and care for ourselves, at least to some extent, we can make others the object of our love meditation. First we take someone we like to be the object of our meditation; then, successively, someone neutral to us, someone we love, and someone we dislike very much. In the *Vishuddhimagga,* Buddhaghosa advises us to start with someone we like, because it is easier to offer our mind of love to such a person. He uses the example of lighting a fire. First we ignite some straw. Once the straw is burning, we add small sticks. Once the small sticks have caught fire, we add small logs. Once those have caught fire, we add larger logs until even damp or green logs will burn. But if we try to start the fire with damp logs, we will not succeed.

"May he/she be peaceful, happy, and light in body and in spirit. May he/she be free from injury. May he/she live in safety. May he/she be free from anger, disturbance, fear, worry, and anxiety." As you concentrate on another person as the object of your love meditation, if she lives east of you, send your energy to the east. If she is sitting to your right, extend your energy to the right. Surround her with the energy of love. Even if she is not in need of your love, practice this way. Dwell in deep concentration. Because you know how to love yourself, you have the capacity to offer love to someone you like. Look deeply into her five skandhas — body, feelings, perceptions, mental formations, and consciousness. This practice is quite easy.

Once you succeed with the meditation on someone you like, select someone neutral to you to be the object of your meditation, someone you neither love nor hate, perhaps the mailman or the electrician. Even if you feel a little positively or negatively toward him, it is not exactly love or hatred. One neutral person can represent millions of others. Suppose you want to extend your love to the Bosnians. Take as the object of meditation one Bosnian man or woman you can visualize. Look deeply and visualize his body, feelings, perceptions, mental formations, and consciousness, and you will see the situation of his whole nation. If you can understand him, you can love and understand all the people of Bosnia. When you say, "May all beings be happy," if there is no clear or concrete subject, your wish may be too vague. It is easier to focus on one person and say, "May he and all those like him be safe and free from injury." Then your love will take hold in a real way. Love meditation is not wishful thinking. It is an authentic practice. Looking deeply, you radiate the energy of mindfulness onto the object of your meditation and illuminate it. True seeing always gives rise to true love.

A few months later, when you feel ready to move to the next stage of practice, take someone you love to be the object of your meditation. It can even be the person most dear to you. "May she be peaceful, happy, and light in body and spirit. May she be safe and free from injury. May she be free from anger, afflictions, fear, and anxiety." This practice is very sweet, and that is why the *Vishuddhimagga* warns that it can have pitfalls. You can lose concentration while meditating on someone to whom you are too deeply attached.

Finally, meditate on someone you consider to be your enemy, someone whom just thinking about makes you angry. Put yourself in his place and give rise to the thought, "May he be peaceful, happy, and light in body and spirit." If you are not yet able to love yourself, you will not be able to love your enemy. But when you are able to love yourself, you can love anyone. When you do this, you will see that your so-called enemy is not more or less than a human being who is suffering. "May he be safe and free from injury." During the Vietnam War, I meditated on the Vietnamese soldiers, praying they would not be killed in battle. But I also meditated on the American soldiers and felt a very deep sympathy for them. I knew that they had been sent far away from home to kill or be killed, and I prayed for their safety. That led to a deep aspiration that the war would end and allow Vietnamese and Americans to live in peace. Once that aspiration was clear, there was only one path to take — to work for the end of the war. When you practice love meditation, you have to take that path. As soon as you see that the person you call your enemy is also suffering, you will be ready to love and accept him. The idea of "enemy" vanishes and is replaced by the reality of someone who is suffering and needs our love and compassion.

"May I be able to recognize and touch the seeds of joy and

happiness in myself." First, learn to touch and identify the seeds of happiness and joy in yourself. When you are successful, even occasionally, continue with others. Even if the other person is extremely unhappy, you know that she has the seeds of joy and happiness in her. After you learn to water those seeds in yourself, you know how to do that same in her. Through your words, your glance, the touch of your hand, your loving care, you will be able to help her touch those seeds, and that will help her, and it will help you also.   — *Teachings on Love*

BEGINNING ANEW

Do you have someone to love? We all want to love and be loved. If you do not have anyone to love, your heart may dry up. Love brings happiness to ourselves and to the ones we love.

You think you can change the world, but do not be too naïve. You may be able to give beautiful talks about harmony, but if you are not prepared, you will not be able to put your words into practice. We want to go out and share what we have learned. But if we do not practice mindful breathing to untie the knots of pain in ourselves — the knots of anger, sadness, jealousy, and irritation — what can we teach others? We must understand and practice the teaching in our daily lives. People need to hear how we have to be able to overcome our own suffering and the irritations in our own heart. When we talk about the Dharma, our words need to have energy. That is not possible if our words come only from ideas, theories, or even sutras. We can only teach what we have experienced ourselves.

Eight years ago I organized a retreat for American veterans of the Vietnam War. Many of the men and women at that retreat felt very guilty for what they had done and witnessed, and I knew I had to find a way of beginning anew that could help them transform. One veteran told me that when he was in Vietnam, he rescued a girl who had been wounded and was about to die. He pulled her into his helicopter, but he was not able to save her life. She died looking straight at him, and he has never forgotten her eyes. She had a hammock with her, because as a guerilla, she slept in the forest at night. When she died, he kept the hammock and would not let it go. Sometimes when we suffer, we have to cling to our suffering. The hammock symbolized all his suffering, all his shame.

During the retreat, the veterans sat in a circle and spoke about their suffering, some for the first time. In a retreat for veterans, a lot of love and support is needed. Some veterans would not do walking meditation, because it reminded them too much of walking in the jungles of Vietnam, where they could step on a mine or walk into an ambush at any time. One man walked far behind the rest of us so that if anything happened he would be able to get away quickly. Veterans live in that kind of psychological environment.

On the last day of the retreat, we held a ceremony for the deceased. Each veteran wrote the names of those he or she knew had died, and placed the list on an altar we constructed. I took a willow leaf and used it to sprinkle water on the names and also on the veterans. Then we did walking meditation to the lake and held a ceremony for burning the suffering. That veteran still did not want to give up his hammock, but finally he put it on the fire. It burned, and all the guilt and suffering in his heart also burned up. We have taken one step, two steps, three steps on the path of transformation. We have to continue on that path.

Another veteran told us that almost everyone in his platoon had been killed by the guerrillas. Those who survived were so angry that they baked cookies with explosives in them and left them alongside the road. When some Vietnamese children saw them, they ate the cookies, and the explosives went off. They were rolling around the ground in pain. Their parents tried to save their lives, but there was nothing they could do. That image of the children rolling on the ground dying because of the explosives in the cookies was so deeply ingrained on this veteran's heart, that now, twenty years later, he still could not sit in the same room with children. He was living in hell. After he had told this story, I gave him the practice of Beginning Anew.

Beginning Anew is not easy. We have to transform our hearts and our minds in very practical ways. We may feel ashamed, but shame is not enough to change our heart. I said to him, "You killed five or six children that day? Can you save the lives of five or six children today? Children everywhere in the world are dying because of war, malnutrition, and disease. You keep thinking about the five or six children that you killed in the past, but what about the children who are dying now? You still have your body, you still have your heart, you can do many things to help children who are dying in the present moment. Please give rise to your mind of love, and in the months and years that are left to you, do the work of helping children." He agreed to do it, and it has helped him transform his guilt.

Beginning Anew is not to ask for forgiveness. Beginning Anew is to change your mind and heart, to transform the ignorance that brought about wrong actions of body, speech, and mind, and to help you cultivate your mind of love. Your shame and guilt will disappear, and you will begin to experience the joy of being alive. All wrongdoings arise in the mind. It is through the mind that wrongdoings can disappear.

— Teachings on Love

THE BUDDHA'S SMILE

All pairs of opposites are created by our own minds from our store consciousness. We make happiness and suffering into an enormous struggle. If we could only penetrate the true face of reality all our sorrows and misfortunes would vanish like smoke, and we would indeed "overcome ill-being."

Look at the Buddha's smile. It is completely peaceful and

compassionate. Does that mean that the Buddha does not take your and my suffering seriously? The Buddha sent Bodhisattva Sadaparibhuta to inform us that the Buddha does not look down at anyone, because every being will become a Buddha.

Maybe my response to the Buddha's smile is caused by a childish sense of inferiority — it certainly does not arise from a feeling of self-respect. It is easy for us to feel insignificant, clumsy, and stupid before the Buddha, who sees nirvana and *samsara* as mere flickers of emptiness. Yet I am certain that the Buddha feels compassion for us, not because we suffer but because we do not see the path, and that is the cause of our suffering.

Since I was a young man, I've tried to understand the nature of compassion. But what little compassion I've learned has come not from intellectual investigation but from my actual experience of suffering. I am not proud of my suffering any more than a person who mistakes a rope for a snake is proud of his fright. My suffering has been a mere rope, a mere drop of emptiness so insignificant that it should dissolve like mist at dawn. But it has not dissolved, and I am almost unable to bear it. Doesn't the Buddha see my suffering? How can he smile? Love seeks a manifestation — romantic love, motherly love, patriotic love, love of humanity, love for all beings.

When you love someone you feel anxious for him or her and want them to be safe and nearby. You cannot simply put your loved ones out of your thoughts. When the Buddha witnesses the endless suffering of living beings, he must feel deep concern. How can he just sit there and smile? But think about it. It is we who sculpt him sitting and smiling, and we do it for a reason. When you stay up all night worrying about your loved one, you are so attached to the phenomenal world that you may not be able to see the true face of reality. A physician who accurately understands her patient's condition does not sit and obsess over a thousand different explanations or anxieties as the patient's family might. The doctor knows that the patient will recover, and so she may smile even while the patient is still sick. Her smile is not unkind; it is simply the smile of one who grasps the situation and does not engage in unnecessary worry. How can I put into words the true nature of Great Compassion?

When we begin to see that black mud and white snow are neither ugly nor beautiful, when we can see them without discrimination or duality, then we begin to grasp Great Compassion. In the eyes of Great Compassion, there is neither left nor right, friend nor enemy, close nor far. Don't think that Great Compassion is lifeless. The energy of Great Compassion is radiant and wondrous. In the eyes of Great Compassion, there is no separation between subject and object, no separate self. Nothing that can disturb Great Compassion.

If a cruel and violent person disembowels you, you can smile and look at him with love. It is his upbringing, his situation, and his ignorance that cause him to act so mindlessly. Look at him — the one who is bent on your destruction and heaps injustice upon you — with eyes of love and compassion. Let compassion pour from your eyes and don't let a ripple of blame or anger rise up in your heart. He commits senseless crimes against you and makes you suffer because he cannot see the way to peace, joy, or understanding.

If some day you receive news that I have died because of someone's cruel actions, know that I died with my heart at peace. Know that in my last moments I did not succumb to anger. We must never hate another being. If you can give rise to this awareness, you will be able to smile. Remembering me, you will continue on our path. You will have a refuge that no one can take from you. No one will be able to disturb your faith, because that faith does not rely on anything in the phenomenal world. Faith and love are one and can only emerge when you penetrate deeply the empty nature of the phenomenal world, when you can see that you are in everything and everything is in you.

Long ago I read a story about a monk who felt no anger

toward the cruel king who had chopped off the monk's ear and pierced his skin with a knife. When I read that, I thought that the monk must be some kind of god. That was because I did not yet know the nature of Great Compassion. The monk had no anger to hold back. All he had was a heart of love. There is nothing to prevent us from being like that monk. Love teaches that we can all live like the Buddha.

— *Fragrant Palm Leaves*

THE ANCIENT TREE

(*Written as a memorial to Nhat Chi Mai, my student who immolated herself for peace on May 16, 1967.* — Thich Nhat Hanh)

In a deep forest in the highlands stood an ancient tree. No one knew how many thousands of years it had lived. Its trunk was so large that the arm spans of eighteen people could not embrace it; great roots pushed up through the ground and spread to a radius of fifty meters. The earth beneath the tree's shadow was unusually cool. Its bark was as hard as rock; if you pressed a fingernail against it, pain ran through your finger. Its branches held tens of thousands of nests, sheltering hundreds of thousands of birds, both large and small.

In the morning, when the sun rose, the first rays of light were like a conductor's baton, initiating a mighty symphony, the voices of thousand of birds, a symphony as majestic as the sun dawning behind the summit of the mountain. All the creatures of the mountain and forest arose, either on two feet or four, slowly, in wonder.

In the great tree there was one hole large as a grapefruit from Bien Hoa and twelve meters from the ground. In the hole lay a small brown egg. No one could say if a bird had brought the beautiful egg to the hole. Some thought the egg had not come from a living bird but had been forged by the sacred air of the forest and the life energy of the great tree.

Thirty years passed; the egg remained intact. Some nights, birds would be startled from their sleep by a cloud hovering over the hole and a brilliant light shining there, illuminating an entire corner of the forest. Finally, one night, under a full moon, the egg opened and a strange bird was born. The bird was very little; it gave a small chirp in the cold night. The moon was very bright; the stars were very bright. The tiny bird cried throughout the night. Its cry was neither tragic nor bold; it was a cry of surprise and strangeness. It cried until the sun appeared. The first rays of light opened the symphony; thousands of birds' voices broke forth. From that moment, the little bird cried no more.

It grew quickly. The nuts and grains mother birds brought to the hole were always plenty. Soon the hole in the tree became too small, and the bird had to find another place, much larger, in which to live. It now knew how to fly; it looked for its own food and gathered sticks of straw to cover the floor of its new nest. Strangely, although the egg had been brown, the bird was as white as snow. When it flew, its wingspan was vast, and it moved slowly and very quietly. Often it flew to faraway places where white waterfalls tumbled day and night like the majestic breath of Earth and sky.

Sometimes the bird did not return for several days. When it returned, it lay in its nest all day and night, thoughtfully and quietly. Its two eyes were very bright; they never lost the look of surprise they had from the beginning.

Now, in the ancient forest of Dai Lao, a hermit's small hut stood on the slope of a hill. There a monk had lived for almost fifty years. The bird often flew across Dai Lao Forest; from time to time it saw the monk walking slowly down the path to the spring, holding a water jug in his hand. One day, smoke gently lingered over the roof of the humble hut and an atmosphere of warmth surrounded the hill. The bird saw two monks together on the path leading from the spring to the hut, speaking as they walked. That night the bird remained in Dai Lao Forest. Concealed in the branches of a tree, the bird watched the light of the fire flickering inside the hut, where the two monks conversed through the night.

The bird flew high, high over the ancient forest. For several days it flew back and forth in the sky without landing. Below stood the great tree in the ancient forest; below, the creatures of the mountain and forest were concealed by grass, bushes, and trees. Since the day the bird listened to the exchange between the two monks, its bewilderment grew. Where have I come from and where will I go? How many thousands of years will the great tree stand?

The bird had heard the two monks speak about Time. What is Time? Why has Time brought us here, and why will it take us away? The nut that a bird eats has its own delicious nature. How can I find out the nature of Time? The bird wanted to pick up a small piece of Time and lie quietly with it in its nest for several days to examine its nature. Even if it took months or years to examine, the bird was willing.

The bird flew high, high over the ancient forest. It was like a round balloon drifting in nothingness. The bird felt its nature was as empty as a balloon's. The emptiness of its nature was the ground of its existence, but it was also the cause of the bird's suffering: "Time, if I could find you, certainly I could find myself," thought the bird.

After several days and nights, the bird came to rest quietly in its nest. It had brought back a tiny piece of earth from the Dai Lao Forest. Deep in thought, it picked up the piece of earth to examine it. The monk from the Dai Lao forest had said to his friend, "Time is stilled in Eternity. There Love and Beloved are One. Each blade of grass, each piece of earth, each leaf, is one with that love."

The bird was still unable to find Time. The small token of earth from the Dai Lao Forest revealed nothing. Perhaps the

monk had lied to his friend. Time lies in Love, but where is
Love? The bird remembered the splashing waterfalls endlessly
tumbling in the Northwest Forest. It remembered the days it
listened to the sound of the waterfalls from morning to evening.
The bird had imagined itself tumbling like a waterfall. It played
with the light shining on the water, with the waterfall it caressed
the pebbles and rocks in the streams. In those moments, the bird
felt that it was a waterfall itself, that the sound of endless falling
water came from it.

One noon, flying across the Dai Lao Forest, the bird did not
see the hut. The whole forest had burned; only a pile of ashes
remained where the monk's hut had been. In a panic, the bird
flew around searching. The monk was no longer in the forest.
Where had he gone? Corpses of animals. Corpses of birds. Had
the fire consumed the monk? The bird was bewildered. Time,
where are you? Why do you bring us here and why will you
take us away? The monk said, "Time is stilled in Eternity." If
that is so, perhaps Love has returned the monk to Itself.

Suddenly the bird felt anxious. It flew swiftly back to the
ancient forest. Anguished cries of many birds. Explosions. The
ancient forest, far away, was burning. Faster, faster still, the bird
flew. The fire licked the sky. The fire spread near the great tree.
Hundreds of thousands of birds shrieked in fright.

The fire approached the great tree. The bird fanned the fire
with its wings, hoping to put it out, but the fire burned more
fiercely. The bird sped to the spring, dipped its wings in the
water, and rushed back to shake the water over the forest. The
drops sizzled. It was not enough, not enough. The bird's entire
body soaked in water was not enough to extinguish the fire.

Cries of hundreds of thousands of birds. Screams of young
birds without feathers to fly. The fire began to burn the great
tree. Why was there no rain? Why didn't the downpour that
fell endlessly in the Northwest Forest flow like a waterfall? The
bird let forth a piercing cry. The cry was tragic and passion-
ate and was suddenly transformed into the rushing sound of a

waterfall. All at once, the bird felt the fullness of its existence. Loneliness and emptiness vanished as an illusion. The image of the monk. The image of the sun behind the mountain peak. The image of rushing water falling endlessly through a thousand lifetimes. The cry of the bird was now the full sound of the waterfall. Without anxiety, the bird plunged into the forest fire like a majestic waterfall.

The next morning was calm. The marvelous rays of the sun shone, but there was no symphony, no voices of tens of thousands of birds. Portions of the forest were completely burned. The great tree still stood, but more than half of its branches and leaves were charred. Corpses of large birds, corpses of small birds. The morning forest was silent.

The birds still alive called one another, their voices bewildered. They did not know by what grace the clear sky had suddenly poured forth rain, extinguishing the forest fire the afternoon before. They remembered seeing the bird shaking water from its two wings. They knew it was the white bird from the great tree. They flew everywhere throughout the forest seeking the corpse of the white bird, but they did not find it.

Perhaps the bird had flown away to live in a different forest. Perhaps the bird had been killed by the fire. The great tree, its body covered with wounds, did not say a word. The birds cocked their heads to the sky and began to build new nests in the wounded body of the great tree. Does the great tree miss the child to which sacred mountain air and the life energy of four thousand years had given birth? Bird, where have you gone? Listen to the monk: I believe Time has returned the bird to the Love that is the source of all things.   — *Love in Action*

4

The Path of Return

Buddhist practitioners speak of the Three Jewels (the Buddha, the Dharma, and the Sangha) in which we take refuge. We all need a place in our spiritual life to which we can return. But ultimately there is only one thing we can rely on. That is our practice. Buddha (the Awakened One), Dharma (the teachings of understanding and love given by the Awakened Ones), and Sangha (the community that practices understanding and love): these are three jewels to be cultivated by us in our daily practice. Once we cultivate them in ourselves we have a path of return to our true home.

When Thây came to the West he made friends with many Christian practitioners and learned the value of their faith through the way they practiced it. He also met many young people of Vietnamese descent who had spent much of their young lives in the West. Thây inspires people to return to their roots. Just like a tree, a human being needs to have roots in his or her culture and spiritual tradition. If we do not have these roots we can wander like ghosts, looking for what is missing from our life without ever being able to find it. Thây says that all religious traditions have their jewels. Our understanding of faiths other than our own can help us return to and see more deeply into the faith we were brought up in.

But our true home is not the safety of a particular belief or ideology. Nor is it the safety of a bank account, a house, car, family, or employment. Our true home is the solidity and freedom of our mind, cultivated in the context of a community. Thây has told us many times that the new millennium is a time for us to cease to live as individuals. For the last two hundred years we have cultivated individualism to the maximum degree, and this has brought separation and suffering in its train. Now we have to find new ways of living and acting together. When we look we must learn to look with the eyes of our community; when we act we must act with the hands of our community; and when we decide we must decide with the insight of our community.

The poem which opens this section, "The Fruit of Awareness Is Ripe," was written before Thây left Vietnam in 1966. It was written for Thây Thanh Van, a young monk who had been appointed director of the School of Youth for Social Services and who was later killed during the war. Thây Thanh Van was still very young when he took on this responsibility. Here Thây identifies himself with his young disciple. The poem is a declaration that Thây and his disciple will never be able to turn back on the path of succoring our world.

Thây has described a dream in which he was shown all the suffering which he had been through in this life and told he would have to go through it again. In the dream he hesitated, but only for a moment, and then declared, "We are not afraid." In the dream he was not alone but with his younger brother. To me the younger brother signifies the Sangha, and what Thây wants to say is that he and the Sangha are not afraid to go through this suffering in order to learn from it and bring relief to others.

—Sister Annabel Laity

THE FRUIT OF AWARENESS IS RIPE

My youthful years,
a green unripe plum.
Your teeth left a mark on it
which turned into a tiny wound.
Your teeth shuddered at their roots,
and always remember it,
always remember it.

But when I knew how to love
the door of my heart opened wide before the wind.
Reality was calling out for revolution.
The fruit was already ripe.
That door
could never be closed again.

Fire,
fire consumes this century,
leaving its mark on the uninhabited mountains
    and forests.
The wind howls past my ears.
The snowstorm writhes in the sky.
The wounds of winter lie there, unable to forget
    the cold steel blade,
restless, tossing and turning,
smarting,
in the deep night.
                    (Newly translated by Sister Annabel Laity)
                        — *Call Me by My True Names*

THE BUDDHA'S HEART

Many people regard Buddhism as a religion, but if we say that
it is a way of life, we may be closer to the truth. Life is the art

of bringing happiness to ourselves and others. If we ourselves are not happy, we cannot make others happy, and if others are not happy, we cannot be truly happy either. To practice the art of bringing happiness to ourselves and others, we need to have faith and confidence in something that we find true and beautiful, that accords with the truth, and that can be a foundation for true and lasting happiness. Because we need such faith, Buddhism is also called a religion. Faith here does not mean faith in a creator god or a metaphysical first principle, the existence of which we cannot really prove. Faith here means confidence in something beautiful and true that can bring about happiness and that we can actually touch.

— For a Future To Be Possible

Buddha was not a god. He was a human being like you and me, and he suffered just as we do. If we go to the Buddha with our hearts open, he will look at us, his eyes filled with compassion, and say, "Because there is suffering in your heart, it is possible for you to enter my heart."

The layman Vimalakirti said, "Because the world is sick, I am sick. Because people suffer, I have to suffer." This statement was also made by the Buddha. Please don't think that because you are unhappy, because there is pain in your heart, that you cannot go to the Buddha. It is exactly because there is pain in your heart that communication is possible. Your suffering and my suffering are the basic condition for us to enter the Buddha's heart, and for the Buddha to enter our hearts.

For forty-five years, the Buddha said, over and over again, "I teach only suffering and the transformation of suffering." When we recognize and acknowledge our own suffering, the Buddha — which means the Buddha in us — will look at it, discover what has brought it about, and prescribe a course of action that can transform it into peace, joy, and liberation. Suffering is the means the Buddha used to liberate himself, and it is also the means by which we can become free.

The ocean of suffering is immense, but if you turn around, you can see the land. The seed of suffering in you may be strong, but don't wait until you have no more suffering before allowing yourself to be happy. When one tree in the garden is sick, you have to care for it. But don't overlook all the healthy trees. Even while you have pain in your heart, you can enjoy the many wonders of life — the beautiful sunset, the smile of a child, the many flowers and trees. To suffer is not enough. Please don't be imprisoned by your suffering.

If you have experienced hunger, you know that having food is a miracle. If you have suffered from the cold, you know the preciousness of warmth. When you have suffered you know how to appreciate the elements of paradise that are present. If you dwell only in your suffering, you will miss paradise. Don't ignore your suffering, but don't forget to enjoy the wonders of life, for your sake and for the benefit of many beings.

I grew up in a time of war. There was destruction all around — children, adults, values, a whole country. As a young person, I suffered a lot. Once the door of awareness has been opened, you cannot close it. The wounds of war in me are still not healed. There are nights I lie awake and embrace my people, my country, and the whole planet with my mindful breathing.

Without suffering, you cannot grow. Without suffering, you cannot get the peace and joy you deserve. Please don't run away from your suffering. Embrace it and cherish it. Go to the Buddha, sit with him, and show him your pain. He will look at you with loving-kindness, compassion, and mindfulness, and show you ways to embrace your suffering and look deeply into it. With understanding and compassion, you will be able to heal the wounds in your heart, and the wounds in the world. The Buddha called suffering a Holy Truth, because your suffering has the capacity of showing us the path to liberation. Embrace your suffering, and let it reveal to you the way to peace.

— The Heart of the Buddha's Teaching

OUR TRUE HOME

The appellation "Buddha" comes from the root of the verb *budh* — which means to wake up, to understand, to know what is happening in a very deep way. In knowing, understanding, and waking up to reality, there is mindfulness, because mindfulness means seeing and knowing what is happening. Whether our seeing is deep or superficial depends on our degree of awakening. In each of us, the seed of Buddha, the capacity to wake up and understand, is called Buddha nature. It is the seed of mindfulness, the awareness of what is happening in the present moment. If I say, "A lotus for you, a Buddha to be," it means, "I see clearly the Buddha nature in you." It may be difficult for you to accept that the seed of Buddha is in you, but we all have the capacity for faith, awakening, understanding, and awareness, and that is what is meant by Buddha nature. There is no one who does not have the capacity to be a Buddha.

But the treasure we are looking for remains hidden to us. Stop being like the man in the *Lotus Sutra* who looked all over the world for the gem that was already in his pocket. Come back and receive your true inheritance. Don't look outside yourself for happiness. Let go of the idea that you don't have it. It is available within you.

How can we live so that the seeds of happiness in us are watered every day? That is the cultivation of joy, the practice of love. We can practice these things easily when we have the energy of mindfulness. But without mindfulness, how can we see the beautiful rice fields? How can we feel the delightful rain? Breathing in, I know the rain is falling. Breathing out, I smile to the rain. Breathing in, I know that rain is a necessary part of life. Breathing out, I smile again. Mindfulness helps us regain the paradise we thought we had lost.

We want to return to our true home, but we are in the habit of running away. We want to sit on a lotus flower, but instead we sit on burning charcoal, and we want to jump off. If we sit firmly in the present moment, it is as though we are sitting on a lotus. The Buddha is always represented as sitting peacefully on a lotus flower, because he was always at home. He didn't need to run anymore. To enjoy sitting in the present moment is called "just sitting" or "non-action." Venerable Thich Quang Duc [the Vietnamese monk who immolated himself in 1963 to call attention to the suffering of his people] was able to sit peacefully even while fire was blazing all around him. He was burning, but he was still sitting on a lotus. That is the ultimate capacity to sit peacefully in any circumstance, knowing that nothing is lost.

The capacity to feel at peace anywhere is a positive seed. The energy to run away is not. If we practice mindfulness, whenever the energy of wanting to run away arises, we can smile at it and say, "Hello, my old friend, I recognize you." The moment we recognize any habit energy, it loses a little of its power.

It isn't necessary to run away or abandon our present home and look for an illusory home, a so-called paradise that is really just a shadow of happiness. When we produce faith, energy, mindfulness, concentration, and insight in our power plants, we realize that our true home is already filled with light and power.
— The Heart of the Buddha's Teaching

THE RAFT IS NOT THE SHORE

The Buddha regarded his own teaching as a raft to cross the river and not as an absolute truth to be worshipped or clung to. He said this to prevent rigid dogmatism or fanaticism from taking root. Ideological inflexibility is responsible for so much of the conflict and violence in the world. According to Buddhist teaching, knowledge itself can be an obstacle to true understanding, and views can be a barrier to insight. Clinging to views can prevent us from arriving at a deeper, more profound understanding of reality. Buddhism urges us to transcend even

our own knowledge if we wish to advance on the Path of
Awakening.

Openness and tolerance are not merely ways to deal with
people in daily life; they are truly gateways for the realization
of the Way. According to Buddhism, if we do not continue
to expand the boundaries of our understanding, we will be
imprisoned by our views and unable to realize the Way.

In the *Sutra of One Hundred Parables,* the Buddha tells
the story of a young merchant and his son. The merchant, a
widower, loved his son dearly, but lost him due to the lack of
wisdom. One day, while the man was away, his little boy was
kidnapped by a gang of bandits, who razed the entire village
before fleeing. When the young merchant returned home, he
found the charred remains of a child near where his house had
been, and in his suffering and confusion, mistook the charred
remains for his own son. He cried unceasingly, arranged a cre-
mation ceremony, and then carried the bag of ashes with him
day and night, tied around his neck. A few months later, his
little boy was able to escape from the bandits and find his way
home. At midnight, he knocked on the door of his father's rebuilt house, but the father, thinking that some mischievous boy
was ridiculing him, refused to open the door. The boy knocked
and knocked, but the merchant clung to his view that his boy
was dead, and eventually his son had to go away. This father
who loved too much lost his son forever.

The Buddha said that when we are attached to views, even if
the truth comes to our house and knocks on our door, we will
refuse to let it in. To inflexibly embrace a view and regard it as
fixed truth is to end the vital process of inquiry and awakening.
The Buddha's teachings are a *means* of helping people. They are
not an *end* to worship or fight over.

Clinging fanatically to an ideology or a doctrine not only prevents us from learning but also creates bloody conflicts. The
worst enemies of Buddhism are fanaticism and narrowness.
Religious and ideological wars have marred the landscape of

human history for millennia. Holy wars do not have a place in Buddhism, because killing destroys the value of Buddhism itself. The destruction of lives and moral values during the Vietnam War was very much the fruit of fanaticism and narrowness. The Order of Interbeing was born during that situation of utmost suffering, like a lotus flower arising from a sea of fire.

— Interbeing

THE THREE JEWELS

I take refuge in the Buddha,
the one who shows me the way in this life.

I take refuge in the Dharma,
the way of understanding and love.

I take refuge in the Sangha,
the community that lives in harmony and awareness.

Taking refuge in Buddha, Dharma, and Sangha is a fundamental practice in Buddhism. These are universal values that transcend sectarian and cultural boundaries. When we were in our mother's womb, we felt secure, protected from heat, cold, hunger, and other difficulties. To seek for refuge means to look for a place like that that is safe, a place we can rely on.

Faith in Buddhism does not mean accepting a theory that we have not personally verified. The Buddha encouraged us to see for ourselves. Taking refuge in the Three Jewels is not blind faith; it is the fruit of our practice. At first, our Buddha may be a book we've read, our Dharma a few encouraging words we've heard, and our Sangha a community we've visited once or twice. But as we continue to practice, the Buddha, the Dharma, and the Sangha reveal themselves to us more fully.

Faith is important for all religions. Some people say, "If we believe in God and it turns out that He does exist, we'll be safe. And if He doesn't, we won't have lost anything." Theologians speak of a "leap of faith," like a child jumping off the table into the arms of his father. The child is not one hundred percent sure his father will catch him, but he has enough faith to jump. In Buddhism, our faith is concrete, not blind, not a leap. It is formed by our own insight and experience. When we take refuge in the Buddha, we express trust in our capacity to walk in the direction of beauty, truth, and deep understanding, based on our experience of the efficacy of the practice. When we take refuge in the Dharma, we enter the path of transformation, the path to end suffering. When we take refuge in the Sangha, we focus our energies on building a community that dwells in mindfulness, harmony, and peace. When we touch these Three Jewels directly and experience their capacity to bring about transformation and peace, our faith is strengthened even further. The Three Jewels are not notions. They are our life.

During the Buddha's last months, he always taught, "Take refuge in yourselves, not in anything else. In you are Buddha, Dharma, and Sangha. Don't look for things that are far away. Everything is in your own heart. Be an island unto yourself." Whenever you feel confused, angry, or lost, if you practice mindful breathing and return to your island of self, you will be in a safe place filled with warm sunlight, cool shade trees, and beautiful birds and light. Buddha is our mindfulness. Dharma is our conscious breathing. Sangha is our Five Aggregates (the components of our self) working in harmony.

If I am ever in an airplane and the pilot announces that the plane is about to crash, I will practice mindful breathing while reciting the Three Refuges. When you receive bad news I hope you will do the same. But don't wait until a critical moment to go back to your island of self. Go back each day by living mindfully. If the practice becomes a habit, when difficulties arise, it will be easy for you to touch the Three Jewels in yourself.

Walking, breathing, sitting, and eating mindfully are all ways to take refuge. This is not blind faith. It is faith based on your real experience.   — *The Heart of the Buddha's Teaching*

THE AVATAMSAKA REALM

The *Avatamsaka Sutra* is one of the most beautiful Buddhist scriptures. Avatamsaka means "flower ornament, garland, or wreath," or "decorating the Buddha with flowers." Isn't the Buddha beautiful enough? Why do we have to decorate him with flowers? The Buddha in this sutra is not just a person. He is more than a person.

The historical Buddha, Shakyamuni, was born twenty-six hundred years ago in Kapilavastu, got married, had a child, left his family to practice, got enlightened, became a well-known teacher, helped many people, and died in Kusinagara at the age of eighty. One day, a disciple of his named Anuradha was walking along the streets of Shravasti, when he was stopped by a group of monks from another sect. The monks asked him, "Will the Buddha exist after his death or cease to exist after his death?" During the lifetime of the Buddha, many people made efforts like that to try to understand the real Buddha. Anuradha told them he did not know. Then, when he returned to the Jeta Grove and reported to the Buddha what had happened, the Buddha told him, "It is difficult to grasp the Buddha. When you see the Buddha in form, feelings, and perceptions, can you identify the Buddha through these things?" Anuradha replied, "No, Lord." Then the Buddha asked, "Can you find the Buddha apart from form, perceptions, mental formations?" "No, Lord," he responded. The Buddha said, "I am in front of you and yet you cannot grasp me. How do you expect to get hold of me after I pass away?" The Buddha called himself *Tathagata*, "coming from suchness (reality as it is)," "going to suchness," or "one who comes from nowhere and goes nowhere," because suchness cannot be confined to coming and going.

There are many stories like this in the scriptures. The Buddha is more than form. He is the living teaching. When you practice the way of the Buddha, you are transformed, and you are with the Buddha all the time.

Before his passing away, the Buddha told his monks, "My friends, this is only my physical body. My Dharma body will be with you for as long as you continue to practice. Take refuge in the Dharma. Take refuge in the island of self. The Buddha is there." His statement is very clear. If you touch the living Dharma body (*Dharmakaya*), you will not complain that you were born more than twenty-five hundred years after the Buddha and have no chance to see him or study with him. The *Dharmakaya* of the Buddha is always present, always alive. Wherever there is compassion and understanding, the Buddha is there, and we can see and touch him. Buddha as the living Dharma is sometimes called *Vairochana*. He is made of light, flowers, joy, and peace, and we can walk with him, sit with him, and take his hand. As we enter the realm of Avatamsaka, it is Vairochana Buddha we encounter.

In the Avatamsaka realm there is a lot of light. The Buddha and the bodhisattvas are all made of light. Let yourself be touched by the light, which is the enlightenment of the Buddha. Beams of light shining in every direction are pouring out from the pores of every enlightened being there. In the Avatamsaka realm, you become light, and you begin to emit light also. Allow yourself to be transformed by the light. Mindfulness is light. When you practice walking meditation alone, enjoying each step deeply, you emit the light of mindfulness, joy, and peace. Every time I see you walking like that, I am struck by one of the beams of light you are emitting, and suddenly I come back to the present moment. Then I, too, begin to walk slowly and deeply, enjoying each step. In the same way, you can allow yourself to be touched by the beams of light that are everywhere in the Avatamsaka realm. When you do, you will become a bodhisattva emanating light also. Let us enter the Avatamsaka realm together and enjoy it. Later, we can open the door for others to come, too.

From any point in the cosmos, people can touch us wherever we are and wherever they are. We are not at all confined by time and space. We penetrate everywhere; we are everywhere. Whenever someone touches something with deep mindfulness, deep looking, he or she will touch us. It may sound strange, but in the Avatamsaka world, it is always that way.

Whenever I touch a flower, I touch the sun and yet I do not get burned. When I touch the flower, I touch a cloud without flying to the sky. When I touch the flower, I touch my consciousness, your consciousness, and the great planet Earth at the same time. This is the Avatamsaka realm. The miracle is possible because of insight into the nature of interbeing. If you really touch one flower deeply, you touch the whole cosmos. The cosmos is neither one nor many. When you touch one, you touch many, and when you touch many, you touch one. Like Shakyamuni Buddha, you can be everywhere at the same time. Think of your child or your beloved touching you now. Look more deeply, and you will see yourself as multitudes, penetrating everywhere, interbeing with everyone and everything.

I have not been in Vietnam for more than twenty-five years, but several generations of young monks, nuns, and laypeople there have been touching me through my books and tapes, which are handwritten and circulated underground, and also through the practices of walking meditation and looking deeply. Through these things, I have been able to stay in touch with the people, the flowers, the trees, and the waters of Vietnam while touching the people, the flowers, the trees, and the waters of Europe and North America. In fact, just a clap of your hands is enough to touch myriad galaxies. The effect of one sound cannot be measured. Your every look, smile, and word reaches faraway universes and influences every living and non-living being in the cosmos. Everything is touching everything else. Everything is penetrating everything else. That is the world of Avatamsaka, and it is also our world. With deep looking and deep touching, we can transform this world into the world of Avatamsaka. The more we practice looking deeply, the more light is present, the more flowers there are, the more oceans, space, parasols, jewels, and clouds there are. It depends on us.

When you emit light, you help people see, because your light wakes them up.   — *Cultivating the Mind of Love*

THE LIVING BUDDHA

A few years ago, a pro-government group in Ho Chi Minh City spread a rumor that I had passed away from a heart attack. This news caused much confusion inside the country. A Buddhist nun wrote me that the news arrived at her community while she was teaching a class of novices, and the atmosphere in the class sank and one nun passed out. I have been in exile for more than [thirty] years because of my involvement in the peace movement, and I do not know this young nun or the present generation of Buddhist monks and nuns in Vietnam. But life and death is only a fiction, and not very deep; why do you cry, sister? You are studying Buddhism, doing what I am doing. So if you exist, I also exist. What does not exist cannot come into existence and what exists cannot cease to be. Have you realized that, sister? If we cannot bring a speck of dust from "existence" to "non-existence," how can we do that to a human? On Earth, many people have been killed struggling for peace, for human rights, for freedom and social justice, but no one can destroy them. They still exist. Sister, do you think that Jesus Christ, Mahatma Gandhi, Lambrakis, Dr. Martin Luther King, Jr., are "dead people"? No, they are still here. We are they. We carry them in each cell of our bodies. If you ever hear such news again, please smile. Your serene smile will prove that you have attained great understanding and courage. Buddhism and all of humankind expect this of you.

                                                        — *The Sun My Heart*

Human beings cannot live happily and meaningfully without something true, wholesome, and beautiful to believe in. Without faith, we live with no sense of responsibility, and we destroy our own bodies, our souls, our families, and our society. Our own time is an era of lost faith. People have lost faith in God, science, ideals, and ideologies. The older generation wants their children to accept their own faith, but that faith is often vague, and many of them themselves have no steady grasp of it. That is why they are unable to expound the essence of faith so that the younger generation can understand, see, and accept it. In the *Sutra on the White-Clad Disciple,* the Buddha says quite clearly, "The teachings can be seen here right now, their function is to direct in the best direction. They can be approached in order to be directly experienced and someone who has the wisdom to examine them can, by listening to them, understand them." The teachings of the Buddha are only to help us give birth to this faith. Once faith has arisen, we have a new source of energy within us, and with this energy we can live with joy, freshness, and happiness in each moment, knowing how to protect body, mind, and soul, and build a new family and a new society. Our life will begin to have meaning.

All spiritual and religious traditions have the responsibility of initiating and helping develop faith. If we are stuck in old ways of seeing things, we are not able to carry out this responsibility. The people who represent and take responsibility for religious traditions should look at this very carefully. They should not, in the name of tradition, force the younger generation to accept things they cannot experience for themselves, because this will make them turn away from those things altogether. Ours is a scientific age. We cannot force young people to believe in vague, abstract ideas that they cannot experience directly. We need to

go back to something deep in our traditions and rediscover the
best values that have been buried under countless layers of rigid
forms. Only then will we have the insight and the language to
express the true objects of our faith and confidence.

The Dharma is a living reality. Like a great tree that is always
growing, Buddhism continues to develop.

— For a Future To Be Possible

Those who bring Buddhist practice to the West should do so in
this spirit. Since Buddhism is not yet known to most Westerners,
the essence of Buddhism won't have much chance to blossom
in the West if the teachings emphasize form too much. If you
think that the teachings of Buddhism are completely separate
from the other teachings in your society, that is a big mistake.
When I travel in the West to share the teachings of Buddhism,
I often remind people that there are spiritual values in Western
culture and tradition — Judaism, Islam, and Christianity — that
share the essence of Buddhism. When you look deeply into your
culture and tradition, you will discover many beautiful spiritual
values. They are not called Buddhadharma, but they are really
Buddhadharma in their content.

In his last meal, for example, Jesus held up a piece of bread
and shared it with his students, saying, "Friends, eat this bread
which is my flesh. I offer it to you." When he poured the wine,
he said, "Here is my blood. I offer it to you. Drink it." Many
years ago, when I met Cardinal Danielou in Paris, I told him,
"I think Lord Jesus was teaching his students the practice of
mindfulness." In our life, we eat and drink many times a day,
but while doing so, our mind is usually wandering elsewhere,
and what we really eat are our worries, thoughts, and anxieties. Eating in mindfulness is to be in touch with life. Jesus
spoke the way he did so that his students would *really* eat the
bread. The Last Supper was a mindfulness meal. If the disciples could pierce through their distractions and eat one piece
of bread in the present moment with their whole being, isn't

that Buddhadharma? Words like "mindfulness" or "meditation" may not have been used, but the fact that thirteen people were sitting and eating together in mindfulness is surely the practice of Buddhism. Vietnamese King Tran Nhan Tong once said that eating a meal, drinking water, and using the toilet are all Buddhadharma. Buddhadharma is not something different from so-called non-Buddhadharma.

— *The Diamond That Cuts through Illusion*

The Buddha is not found only on Gridhrakuta, the Vulture Peak. If you were to hear on the radio that the Buddha is going to reappear on Gridhrakuta Mountain and the public is invited to join him for walking meditation, all the seats on all the airplanes to India would be booked, and you might feel frustrated, because you want to go, also. Even if you were lucky enough to get a seat on that plane, it still might not be possible for you to enjoy practicing walking meditation with the Buddha. There would be *so* many people, most of whom don't know how to practice breathing in and out and dwelling in the present moment while walking. What is the use of going there?

Look deeply at your intention. Do you want to fly halfway around the world so that later you can say you were with the Buddha? Many people want to do just that. They arrive at a place of pilgrimage, unable to be in the here and the now. After a few minutes of seeing the place, they rush to the next place. They take pictures to prove they were there, and they are eager to return home to show their friends. "I was there. I have proof. That is me standing beside the Buddha." That would be the desire of many of the people who would go there. They are not able to walk with the Buddha. They are not able to be in the here and the now. They only want to say, "I was there, and this is me standing beside the Buddha." But it is not true. They were not there. And that is not the Buddha. "Being there" is a concept, and the Buddha that you see is a mere appearance.

You cannot photograph the real Buddha, even if you have a very expensive camera.

If you don't have the opportunity to fly to India, please practice walking at home, and you can really hold the hand of the Buddha while you walk. Just walk in peace and happiness and the Buddha is there with you. The one who flies to India and returns with his photo taken with the Buddha has not seen the real Buddha. You have the reality; he has only a sign. Don't run around looking for photo opportunities. Touch the real Buddha. He is available. Take his hand and practice walking meditation. When you can touch the ultimate dimension, you walk with the Buddha. The wave does not need to die to become water. She is already water. Live every moment of your life deeply, and while walking, eating, drinking, and looking at the morning star, you touch the ultimate dimension.

                    — *The Heart of the Buddha's Teaching*

JESUS AND BUDDHA

I always think that to be able to look into the eyes of the one true Master is worth one hundred years studying His doctrine, His teaching. In Him you have a direct example of enlightenment, of life, while in others you have only a shadow, which may help you also, but not directly. As the Buddha says, "My doctrine is only a raft helping to bring you over to the other shore, not ultimate reality; you shouldn't worship it."

How do you look into the eyes of Jesus or Buddha? Well, there's no how. It's like asking, How do I look at you? How do I look at a branch of a tree? The problem is not how, but the subject who does the looking. Because if you put in front of people one thing, and you have many people come and look at it, they see different things. It depends not only on the thing you exhibit but on the nature and the substance of the one who looks. So when you are in direct touch with reality, you have more chance to break into it rather than when you have just an image of reality; that's the map and not the city, the shadow not the tree, the doctrine and not the savior, life. There are those who look into the eyes of the Buddha, into the eyes of Jesus, but who are not capable of seeing the Buddha or Jesus. I think that is quite hopeless.

We have a number of stories in Buddhist literature of the many people who came from very far in hope that they might be able to see the Buddha. But they could not see the Buddha because of the way they reacted to things they had seen on the way. One such man met a woman who needed help, but he was in such a hurry to see the Buddha that he neglected the child of the helpless widow. Of course he could not see the Buddha. So I say that whether you can see the Buddha or not depends very much on you.

When I spoke of looking into the eyes of Buddha, I was thinking of the Buddha as a human being who is surrounded by a special atmosphere. I notice that great humans bring with them something like a hallowed atmosphere, and when we seek them out, then we feel peace, we feel love, we feel courage.

Maybe only an image can explain this. The Chinese say, "When a sage is born, the water in the river and the plants and trees on the mountains nearby become clearer and more green." It is their way of talking about the milieu that is born at the same time as a holy being.

When a sage is there and you sit near him, you feel light, you feel peace. That is why I said that if you sit close to Jesus and look into His eyes and still don't see Him, that's hopeless, because in such a case you have much more chance to see, to be saved, to get enlightenment, than when you read His teachings. Of course, if He's not there, His teaching is next best.

When I read and hold the scriptures, whether Buddhist or Christian, I always try to be aware of the fact that when the Buddha or Jesus said something, they were saying it to someone or to some group of people. I should understand the circumstances in which they spoke, in order to get into communion with them rather than merely take their saying word for word. I believe that what the Buddha said, what Jesus said, is not as important as the *way* the Buddha or Jesus said it. If you are able to perceive that, you will get close to the Buddha or to Jesus. But if you try to analyze, try to find out the deep meaning of the words without realizing the kind of relationships between the one who spoke and those who listened, I think that you very easily miss not only the point but the man. I think that theologians tend to forget that approach.

— *The Raft Is Not the Shore*

On the altar in my hermitage in France are images of Buddha and Jesus, and every time I light incense, I touch both of them as my spiritual ancestors. I can do this because of contact with these real Christians. When you touch someone who authentically represents a tradition, you not only touch his or her tradition, you also touch your own. This quality is essential for dialogue. When participants are willing to learn from each other, dialogue takes place just by their being together. When those who represent a spiritual tradition embody the essence of their tradition, just the way they walk, sit, and smile speaks volumes about the tradition.

In fact, sometimes it is more difficult to have a dialogue with people in our own tradition than with those of another tradition. Most of us have suffered from feeling misunderstood or even betrayed by those of our own tradition. But if brothers and sisters in the same tradition cannot understand and communicate with each other, how can they communicate with those outside their tradition? For dialogue to be fruitful, we need to live deeply our own tradition and, at the same time, listen deeply to others. Through the practice of deep looking and deep listening, we become free, able to see the beauty and values in our own *and* others' tradition.

Many years ago, I recognized that by understanding your

own tradition better, you also develop increased respect, consideration, and understanding for others. I had had a naïve thought, a kind of prejudice inherited from my ancestors. I thought that because Buddha had taught for forty-five years and Jesus for only two or three, that Buddha must have been a more accomplished teacher. I had that thought because I did not know the teachings of the Buddha well enough.

One day when he was thirty-eight years old, the Buddha met King Prasenajit of Kosala. The king said, "Reverend, you are young, yet people call you 'The Highest Enlightened One.' There are holy men in our country eighty and ninety years old, venerated by many people, yet none of them claims to be the highest enlightened one. How can a young man like you make such a claim?"

The Buddha replied, "Your majesty, enlightenment is not a matter of age. A tiny spark of fire has the power to burn down a whole city. A small poisonous snake can kill you in an instant. A baby prince has the potentiality of a king. And a young monk has the capacity of becoming enlightened and changing the world." We can learn about others by studying ourselves.

For any dialogue between traditions to be deep, we have to be aware of both the positive and negative aspects of our own tradition. In Buddhism, for example, there have been many schisms. One hundred years after the passing of the Buddha, the community of his disciples divided into two parts; within four hundred years, there were twenty schools; and since then, there have been many more. Fortunately, these separations have, for the most part, not been too painful, and the garden of Buddhism is now filled with many beautiful flowers, each school representing an attempt to keep the Buddha's teachings alive under new circumstances. Living organisms need to change and grow. By respecting the differences within our own church and seeing how these differences enrich one another, we are more open to appreciating the richness and diversity of other traditions.

In a true dialogue, both sides are willing to change. We have to appreciate that truth can be received from outside of — not only within — our own group. If we do not believe that, entering into dialogue would be a waste of time. If we think we monopolize the truth and we still organize a dialogue, it is not authentic. We have to believe that by engaging in dialogue with the other person, we have the possibility of making a change within ourselves, that we can become deeper. Dialogue is not a means for assimilation in the sense that one side expands and incorporates the other into its "self." Dialogue must be practiced on the basis of "non-self." We have to allow what is good, beautiful, and meaningful in the other's tradition to transform us.

But the most basic principle of interfaith dialogue is that the dialogue must begin, first of all, within oneself. Our capacity to make peace with another person and with the world depends very much on our capacity to make peace with ourselves. If we are at war with our parents, our family, our society, or our church, there is probably a war going on inside us also, so that the most basic work for peace is to return to ourselves and create harmony among the elements within us — our feelings, our perceptions, and our mental states. That is why the practice of meditation, looking deeply, is so important. We must recognize and accept the conflicting elements that are within us and their underlying causes. It takes time, but the effort always bears fruit. When we have peace within, real dialogue with others is possible.   — *Living Buddha, Living Christ*

LIVING BUDDHA, LIVING CHRIST

There is a science called Buddhology, the study of the life of the Buddha. As a historical person, the Buddha was born in Kapilavastu, near the border between India and Nepal, got married, had one child, left home, practiced many kinds of meditation, became enlightened, and shared the teaching until he died at the age of eighty. But there is also the Buddha within ourselves who transcends space and time. This is the living Buddha, the Buddha of the ultimate reality, the one who transcends all ideas and notions and is available to us at any time. The living Buddha was not born at Kapilavastu, nor did he pass away at Kushinagara.

When speaking about Christ, we also have to know whether we mean the historical Jesus or the living Jesus. The historical Jesus was born in Bethlehem, the son of a carpenter, traveled far from his homeland, became a teacher, and was crucified at the age of thirty-three. The living Jesus is the Son of God who was resurrected and who continues to live. In Christianity, you have to believe in the resurrection or you are not considered a Christian. I am afraid this criterion may discourage some people from looking into the life of Jesus. That is a pity, because we can appreciate Jesus Christ as both a historical door and an ultimate door.

When we look into and touch deeply the life and teaching of Jesus, we can penetrate the reality of God. Love, understanding, courage, and acceptance are expressions of the life of Jesus. God made Himself known to us through Jesus Christ. With the Holy Spirit and the Kingdom of God within Him, Jesus touched the people of his time. He talked with prostitutes and tax collectors, and had the courage to do whatever was needed to heal His society. As the child of Mary and Joseph, Jesus is the Son of woman and man. As someone animated by the energy of the Holy Spirit, He is the Son of God. The fact that Jesus is both the Son of Man and the Son of God is not difficult for a Buddhist to accept. We can see the nature of non-duality in God the Son and God the Father, because without God the Father within Him, the Son could never be. But in Christianity, Jesus is usually seen as the only Son of God. I think it is important to look deeply into every act and every teaching of Jesus during His lifetime, and to use this as a model for our own practice.

Jesus lived exactly as He taught, so studying the life of Jesus is crucial to understanding His teaching. For me, the life of Jesus is His most basic teaching, more important than even faith in the resurrection or faith in eternity.

•

The Buddha was a human being who was awakened and, thereby, no longer bound by the many afflictions of life. But when some Buddhists say that they believe in the Buddha, they are expressing their faith in the wonderful, universal Buddha, not in the teaching of the life of the historical Buddha. They believe in the Buddha's magnificence and feel that is enough. But the examples of the actual lives of the Buddha and of Jesus are most important, because as human beings, they lived in ways that we can live, too.

When we read, "The heavens opened and the Holy Spirit descended upon Him like a dove," we can see that Jesus Christ was already enlightened. He was in touch with the reality of life, the source of mindfulness, wisdom, and understanding within Him, and this made Him different from other human beings. When He was born into a carpenter's family, He was the Son of Man. When He opened His heart, the door of Heaven was opened to Him. The Holy Spirit descended on Him like a dove, and He was manifested as the Son of God — very holy, very deep, and very great. But the Holy Spirit is not just for Jesus alone; it is for all of us. From a Buddhist perspective, who is not the son or daughter of God? Sitting beneath the Bodhi tree, many wonderful, holy seeds within the Buddha blossomed forth. He was human, but, at the same time, he became an expression of the highest spirit of humanity. *When we are in touch with the highest spirit in ourselves, we too are a Buddha, filled with the Holy Spirit, and we become very tolerant, very open, very deep, and very understanding.*

•

Matthew described the Kingdom of God as being like a tiny mustard seed. It means that the seed of the Kingdom of God is within us. If we know how to plant that seed in the moist soil of our daily lives, it will grow and become a large bush on which many birds can take refuge. We do not have to die to arrive at the gates of Heaven. In fact, we have to be truly alive. The practice is to touch life deeply so that the Kingdom of God becomes a reality. This is not a matter of devotion. It is a matter of practice. The Kingdom of God is available here and now. Many passages in the Gospels support this view. We read in the Lord's Prayer that we do not *go* to the Kingdom of God, but the Kingdom of God comes to us: "Thy Kingdom come..." Jesus said, "I am the door." He describes Himself as the door of salvation and everlasting life, the door to the Kingdom of God. Because God the Son is made of the energy of the Holy Spirit, He is the door for us to enter the Kingdom of God.

The Buddha is also described as a door, a teacher who shows us the way in this life. In Buddhism such a special door is deeply appreciated because that door allows us to enter the realm of mindfulness, loving-kindness, peace, and joy. But it is said that there are eighty-four thousand Dharma doors, doors of teaching. If you are lucky enough to find a door, it would not be very Buddhist to say that yours is the only door. In fact, we have to open even more doors for future generations. We should not be afraid of more Dharma doors — if anything, we should be afraid that no more will be opened. It would be a pity for our children and their children if we were satisfied with only the eighty-four thousand doors already available. Each of us, by our practice and our loving-kindness, is capable of opening new Dharma doors. Society is changing, people are changing, economic and political conditions are not the same as they were in the time of the Buddha or Jesus. The Buddha relies on us for the Dharma to continue to develop as a living organism — not a stale Dharma, but a real *Dharmakaya*, a real "body of teaching."   — *Living Buddha, Living Christ*

BORN AGAIN

On Christmas Eve we speak about faith, about energy, about the Holy Spirit. To me, the Holy Spirit is faith, the Holy Spirit is mindfulness; the Holy Spirit is love. The Holy Spirit is already there within us. If we are able to touch it within ourselves and help it to manifest in us, we can cultivate the Holy Spirit the way we cultivate mindfulness.

After having been baptized by John the Baptist in the Jordan River, Jesus went into the wilderness and stayed there for forty days in order to strengthen the Holy Spirit in himself. During those forty days he must have sat and walked, practicing walking meditation and sitting meditation. Unfortunately, the Gospels did not record the way he sat and the way he walked. But Jesus did sit and did walk.

At the time when John baptized him, the sky opened and the Holy Spirit came down to him like a dove and entered into him. It is so described in the Gospels. Jesus went into the wilderness in order to strengthen that energy within him. He then had the energy to perform miracles of nourishing and of healing in his public life.

The Holy Spirit is something to be cultivated, and the seeds of the Holy Spirit are already within you. To be baptized is to have the opportunity to recognize that this Spirit and that energy are already in you. To be baptized is to recognize the Holy Spirit and to touch it within you. When baptism is celebrated, the people make the sign of the cross in order to remind the congregation, the Sangha, the community, of the presence of God, God the Father, God the Son, and God the Holy Spirit.

In the moment of baptizing, the head of the person is submerged into water one, two, three times. The person who is to be baptized will be born from that water and from the Holy Spirit. In the Orthodox tradition, people like to have the whole head submerged into the waters of baptism. But in the Catholic tradition, people may prefer only to pour the blessed water over the head of the person to be baptized. That kind of ritual aims at helping people touch the seed of the Holy Spirit that is already in him or in her. This ritual is undertaken to help someone to be born in his or her spiritual life. A child is born; Jesus is born every time the Holy Spirit in you is touched.

The same thing is true for someone who practices the Dharma. Every time you touch the seed of mindfulness and mindfulness manifests in you, life is possible again. In a state of distraction, body and mind are not together. If you are lost in the future or in the past, you are not alive. But when the seed of mindfulness in you is touched, suddenly you become alive, body and spirit together. You are born again. Jesus is born again. The Buddha is born again.

When you hear the meditation bell, you stop your thinking. You stop what you are saying, and the bell rescues you and brings you back to your true home, where the Holy Spirit and mindfulness are alive. There you are born again; you are born several times a day, thanks to the Sangha surrounding you. This is the practice of resurrection. We die so many times a day. We lose ourselves so many times a day. And thanks to the Sangha and the practice, we also come back to life several times a day. If you don't practice, then when you lose your life every day you have no chance to be reborn again. Redemption and resurrection are neither words nor objects of belief. They are our daily practice. And we practice in such a way that Buddha is born every moment of our daily life, that Jesus Christ is born every moment of our daily life — not only on Christmas day, because every day is Christmas day, every minute is a Christmas minute. The child within us is waiting each minute for us to be born again and again.

You are born in order to die again; this is the fact. If the Sangha, the church, and the teacher are not there, you are likely to die again. You may die for a long time before you have a chance to be reborn again. The Sangha is your chance, your opportunity; the Sangha is your life.

We have to make steady progress in our spiritual life. There are many people who, after having been baptized, will sin and confess, sin and confess, and sin and suffer again. Is there any progress made as a result of that process? If there is not, then we have to transform our situation. We cannot afford to let things go on and on like that. It's a tragedy, and also a comedy. We have to let our faith grow. To help our faith grow, we have to let our love grow. And because our faith and our love continue to grow, our happiness will also grow. If you are not peaceful, and happy and strong, how can you expect to help other people to be happy, and strong, and stable?

So let us sit down together as a group of brothers and sisters, as a Sangha, to practice looking deeply again in our lives and how we conduct them. We are supposed to be born already in our spiritual life. How do we take care of our life so that each time we are born we can grow stronger? If mindfulness is cultivated in our daily life, if concentration and insight are cultivated in our daily life, we become more open, more tolerant, and our faith and love grow stronger within us. And we know that without the Sangha and continuous practice, we cannot grow steadily. Instead, we will be off and on, off and on, up and down, up and down. We arrive nowhere. That is not really a spiritual life.

— Going Home

RECOMMENDATION

(*I wrote this poem in 1965 especially for the young people in the School of Youth for Social Service who risked their lives every day during the war, recommending them to prepare to die without hatred. Some had already been killed violently, and I cautioned the others against hating. Our enemy is our anger, hatred, greed, fanaticism, and discrimination against men. If you die because of violence, you must meditate on compassion in order to forgive those who kill you. When you die realizing*

*this state of compassion, you are truly a child of the Awakened
One. Even if you are dying in oppression, shame, and violence,
if you can smile with forgiveness, you have great power.... On
our path of service, there are moments of pain and loneliness, but when we know that the Buddha sees and knows
us, we feel a great surge of energy, and firm determination to
carry on.* — Thich Nhat Hanh)

> Promise me,
> promise me this day,
> promise me now,
> while the sun is overhead
> exactly at the zenith,
> promise me:

> Even as they
> strike you down
> with a mountain of hatred and violence;
> even as they step on you and crush you
> like a worm,
> even as they
> dismember and disembowel you,
> remember, brother,
> remember:
> man is not our enemy.

> The only thing worthy of you is compassion —
> invincible, limitless, unconditional.
> Hatred will never let you face
> the beast in man.
> One day, when you face this beast alone,
> with your courage intact, your eyes kind,
> untroubled
> (even as no one sees them),
> out of your smile
> will bloom a flower.

And those who love you
will behold you
across ten thousand worlds of birth and dying.

Alone again,
I will go on with bent head,
knowing that love has become eternal.
On the long, rough road,
the sun and the moon
will continue to shine.

— *Call Me by My True Names*

5

The Heart of Practice

The Buddha was asked, "What do you and your disciples practice?" and he replied, "We sit, we walk, and we eat." The questioner continued, "But sir, everyone sits, walks, and eats." The Buddha told him, "When we sit, we know we are sitting. When we walk, we know we are walking. When we eat, we know we are eating."

— *The Long Road Turns to Joy*

Thây always reminds us that our practice of love and compassion has to be authentic and engaged. That is why we have to apply our meditation in daily life. When we are seated in the meditation hall we have the opportunity to face and unravel the real difficulties of our life. Thây has developed two forms of mindfulness trainings to help us apply our meditation to daily life. These trainings help us to see the causes of suffering, and as a result we resolve to live in a different way.

For a new religious order called the Order of Interbeing, which he founded in Vietnam in the 1960s, Thây devised a set of Fourteen Mindfulness Trainings that would serve as its guiding light. These mindfulness trainings were based on the Ten Wholesome Practices, a set of precepts devised by the Tendai school of Buddhism in China. The Ten Wholesome Practices can be analyzed in three parts: wholesome practices of body, of speech, and of mind. Although the Fourteen Mindfulness Train-

ings of the Order of Interbeing are clearly based on the Ten Wholesome Practices, they also go further. They take the essential teachings of Buddhism on non-dualism, non-violence, and non-discrimination and place them in a form that we can practice in our daily lives.

These trainings are relevant to a country at war, but they are also relevant to our own times. Thây has said that once war has broken out there is little you can do. War breaks out because of the way we conduct ourselves when there is no war going on. We should ask ourselves whether the way in which we are living now is taking us on a path to war. Although we may think that living in the United States today we are not making war, nevertheless the economic and political and social aspects of our way of life could be laying down all the right conditions for war. Thus the Fourteen Mindfulness Trainings of the Order of Interbeing are as relevant now as they were during the war in Vietnam. Whoever hears them deeply, whether Buddhist or not, can hardly fail to be moved and nourished by these Trainings. They offer us hope in a wholesome and beautiful way of life in dark times.

After living in Europe and North America and looking deeply into the suffering of our time, Thây saw the need to articulate a set of concise principles of spiritual practice. To this end he devised an additional Five Mindfulness Trainings, an adaptation of the five precepts that the Buddha composed for his followers. They are not presented as commandments telling us what not to do. They declare our awareness of five different aspects of suffering and our determination to act in ways that do not cause these five kinds of suffering. These are the suffering represented by the destruction of life; the suffering caused by exploitation, stealing, and injustice; the suffering that comes from sexual misconduct; the suffering that comes from harsh, untruthful, and condemnatory speech; and the suffering that comes from the consumption of psychological or physical intoxicants.

Hundreds of thousands of meditation practitioners in the world use these Five Mindfulness Trainings to help them on the path of goodness, beauty, and truth. At the end of a meditation retreat they come before the Sangha and declare their aspiration to create true happiness for themselves and others by training in these five ways with the support of the Sangha. More recently the Five Mindfulness Trainings, as presented by Thây, have formed the basis of a six-point Manifesto 2000 published by the UN to guide people in developing a culture of peace and non-violence. Anyone can pledge himself or herself to live by this manifesto, and at the time of this writing more than thirty million have done so.

—Sister Annabel Laity

THE FOURTEEN MINDFULNESS TRAININGS OF THE ORDER OF INTERBEING

I would like to present to you a form of Buddhism that may be accepted here in the West. In the past decades we have been experimenting with this form of Buddhism, and it seems that it may be suitable for our modern society. It is called the Tiep Hien Order, the Order of "Interbeing."

Tiep means "to be in touch." The notion of engaged Buddhism already appears in the word *tiep*. First of all, to be in touch with oneself. In modern society most of us don't want to be in touch with ourselves. We want to be in touch with other things like religion, sports, politics, a book — we want to forget ourselves. Any time we have leisure, we want to invite something else to enter us, opening ourselves to the television and telling the television to come and colonize us. So first of all, "in touch" means in touch with oneself in order to find out the source of wisdom, understanding, and compassion in each of us. Being in touch with oneself is the meaning of meditation, to be aware of what is going on in your body, in your feelings, in our mind. That is the first meaning of *tiep*.

Tiep also means to be in touch with Buddhas and bodhi-sattvas, the enlightened people in whom full understanding and compassion are tangible and effective. Being in touch with one-self means being in touch with this source of wisdom and compassion. . . .

The second part of the meaning of *tiep* is "to continue," to make something more long-lasting. It means that the career of understanding and compassion started by Buddhas and bodhi-sattvas should be continued. This is possible only if we get in touch with our true self, which is like digging deep into the soil until we reach a hidden source of fresh water, and then the well is filled. When we are in touch with our true mind, the source of understanding and compassion will spring out. This is the basis of everything. Being in touch with our true mind is necessary for the continuation of the career started by the Buddhas and bodhisattvas.

Hien means "the present time." We have to be in the present time, because only the present is real, only in the present moment can we be alive. We do not practice for the sake of the future, to be reborn in a paradise, but to be peace, to be compassion, to be joy right now. *Hien* also means "to make real, to manifest, to realize." Love and understanding are not only concepts and words. They must be real things, realized, in oneself and in society. That is the meaning of the word *hien*.

It is difficult to find English words that convey the same meaning as *Tiep Hien*. There is a term from the *Avatamsaka Sutra*, "interbeing," which conveys the spirit, so we have translated Tiep Hien as interbeing. In the sutra it is a compound term which means "mutual" and "to be." Interbeing is a new word in English, and I hope it will be accepted. We have talked about the many in the one, and the one containing the many. In one sheet of paper, we see everything else, the cloud, the forest, the logger. I am, therefore you are. You are, therefore I am. That is the meaning of the word "interbeing." We inter-are.

In the Order of Interbeing, there are two communities. The

Core Community consists of men and women who have taken the vow to observe the Fourteen Trainings of the Order.* Before being ordained as a brother or a sister of the Order of Interbeing, one should practice at least one year in this way. Upon ordination, the person has to organize a community around himself or herself in order to continue the practice. That community is called the Extended Community. This means all those who practice exactly the same way, but have not taken the vow, have not been ordained into the Core Community.

The people who are ordained into the Core community do not have any special sign at all. They don't shave their heads, they do not have a special robe, except occasionally they wear a brown jacket. What makes them different is that they observe a number of rules, one of which is to practice at least sixty days of retreat, days of mindfulness, each year, whether consecutively or divided into several periods. If they practice every Sunday, for instance, they will have fifty-two already. The people in the Extended Community can do that, or more, even if they don't want to be ordained. In the Core Community people can choose to observe celibacy, or lead a family life.

At least once every two weeks, members and friends come together and recite the Fourteen Trainings. . . . Usually trainings begin with admonitions concerning the body, such as "not to kill." The Tiep Hien trainings are in a kind of reverse order — the ones concentrating the mind come first. In Buddhism, the mind is the root of everything else. These then are the trainings of the Order of Interbeing.   — *Being Peace*

---

*Until recently, I have translated the term for these as "precepts." But many Western friends told me that the word "precepts" evokes in them a strong feeling of good and evil; that if they "break" the precepts, they feel great shame. During the time of the Buddha, the word *shila* (precepts) was usually used for these practices, but the word *shiksa* (trainings) was also often used. Since the meaning of the latter is more consistent with the understanding of how to practice them, without an absolute, black-and-white connotation, I have begun translating these practices as Mindfulness Trainings. — *Teachings on Love.*

1

Aware of the suffering created by fanaticism and intolerance, we are determined not to be idolatrous about or bound to any doctrine, theory, or ideology, even Buddhist ones. Buddhist teachings are guiding means to help us learn to look deeply and to develop our understanding and compassion. They are not doctrines to fight, kill, or die for.

2

Aware of the suffering created by attachment to views and wrong perceptions, we are determined to avoid being narrow-minded and bound to present views. We shall learn and practice nonattachment from views in order to be open to others' insights and experiences. We are aware that the knowledge we presently possess is not changeless, absolute truth. Truth is found in life, and we will observe life within and around us in every moment, ready to learn throughout our lives.

3

Aware of the suffering brought about when we impose our views on others, we are committed not to force others, even our children, by any means whatsoever — such as authority, threat, money, propaganda, or indoctrination — to adopt our views. We will respect the right of others to be different and to choose what to believe and how to decide. We will, however, help others renounce fanaticism and narrowness through practicing deeply and engaging in compassionate dialogue.

4

Aware that looking deeply at the nature of suffering can help us develop compassion and find ways out of suffering, we are determined not to avoid or close our eyes before suffering. We are committed to finding ways, including personal contact, images, and sounds, to be with those who suffer, so we can understand their situation deeply and help them transform their suffering into compassion, peace, and joy.

5

Aware that true happiness is rooted in peace, solidity, freedom, and compassion, and not in wealth or fame, we are determined not to take as the aim of our life fame, profit, wealth, or sensual pleasure, nor to accumulate wealth while millions are hungry and dying. We are committed to living simply and sharing our time, energy, and material resources with those in need. We will practice mindful consuming, not using alcohol, drugs, or any other products that bring toxins into our own and the collective body and consciousness.

6

Aware that anger blocks communication and creates suffering, we are determined to take care of the energy of anger when it arises and to recognize and transform the seeds of anger that lie deep in our consciousness. When anger comes up, we are determined not to do or say anything, but to practice mindful breathing or mindful walking and acknowledge, embrace, and look deeply into our anger. We will learn to look with the eyes of compassion at ourselves and at those we think are the cause of our anger.

7

Aware that life is available only in the present moment and that it is possible to live happily in the here and now, we are committed to training ourselves to live deeply each moment of daily life. We will try not to lose ourselves in dispersion or be carried away by regrets about the past, worries about the future, or craving, anger, or jealousy in the present. We will practice mindful breathing to come back to what is happening in the present moment. We are determined to learn the art of mindful living by touching the wondrous, refreshing, and healing elements that are inside and around us, and by nourishing seeds of joy, peace, love, and understanding in ourselves, thus facilitating the work of transformation and healing in our consciousness.

8

Aware that lack of communication always brings separation and suffering, we are committed to training ourselves in the practice of compassionate listening and loving speech. We will learn to listen deeply without judging or reacting and refrain from uttering words that can create discord or cause the community to break. We will make every effort to keep communications open and to reconcile and resolve all conflicts, however small.

9

Aware that words can create suffering or happiness, we are committed to learning to speak truthfully and constructively, using only words that inspire hope and confidence. We are determined not to say untruthful things for the sake of personal interest or to impress people, nor to utter words that might cause division or hatred. We will not spread news that we do not know to be certain nor criticize or condemn things of which we are not sure. We will do our best to speak out about situations of injustice, even when doing so may threaten our safety.

10

Aware that the essence and aim of a Sangha is the practice of understanding and compassion, we are determined not to use the Buddhist community for personal gain or profit or transform our community into a political instrument. A spiritual community should, however, take a clear stand against oppression and injustice and should strive to change the situation without engaging in partisan conflicts.

11

Aware that great violence and injustice have been done to our environment and society, we are committed not to live with a vocation that is harmful to humans and nature. We will do our best to select a livelihood that helps realize our ideal of understanding and compassion. Aware of global economic, political and social realities, we will behave responsibly as consumers and as citizens, not supporting companies that deprive others of their chance to live.

12

Aware that much suffering is caused by war and conflict, we are determined to cultivate nonviolence, understanding, and compassion in our daily lives, to promote peace education, mindful mediation, and reconciliation within families, communities, nations, and in the world. We are determined not to kill and not to let others kill. We will diligently practice deep looking with our Sangha to discover better ways to protect life and prevent war.

13

Aware of the suffering caused by exploitation, social injustice, stealing, and oppression, we are committed to cultivating

loving-kindness and learning ways to work for the well-being
of people, animals, plants, and minerals. We will practice generosity by sharing our time, energy, and material resources with
those who are in need. We are determined not to steal and not
to possess anything that should belong to others. We will respect the property of others, but will try to prevent others from
profiting from human suffering or the suffering of other beings.

14

(For lay members): Aware that sexual relations motivated by
craving cannot dissipate the feeling of loneliness but will create more suffering, frustration, and isolation, we are determined
not to engage in sexual relations without mutual understanding,
love, and a long-term commitment. In sexual relations, we must
be aware of future suffering that may be caused. We know that
to preserve the happiness of ourselves and others, we must respect the rights and commitments of ourselves and others. We
will do everything in our power to protect children from sexual
abuse and to protect couples and families from being broken
by sexual misconduct. We will treat our bodies with respect
and preserve our vital energies (sexual, breath, spirit) for the
realization of our bodhisattva ideal. We will be fully aware of
the responsibility of bringing new lives into the world, and will
meditate on the world into which we are bringing new beings.

(For monastic members): Aware that the aspiration of a
monk or a nun can only be realized when he or she wholly
leaves behind the bonds of worldly love, we are committed
to practicing chastity and to helping others protect themselves.
We are aware that loneliness and suffering cannot be alleviated
by the coming together of two bodies in a sexual relationship,
but by the practice of true understanding and compassion. We
know that a sexual relationship will destroy our life as a monk
or a nun, will prevent us from realizing our ideal of serving
living beings, and will harm others. We are determined not to

suppress or mistreat our body or to look upon our body as only an instrument, but to learn to handle our body with respect. We are determined to preserve vital energies (sexual, breath, spirit) for the realization of our bodhisattva ideal. — *Interbeing*

THE FIVE MINDFULNESS TRAININGS

I have been in the West for thirty years, and for the past ten I have been leading mindfulness retreats in Europe, Australia, and North America. During these retreats, my students and I have heard many stories of suffering, and we have been dismayed to learn how much of this suffering is the result of alcoholism, drug abuse, and similar behaviors that have been passed down from generation to generation.

There is a deep malaise in society. When we put a young person in this society without trying to protect him, he receives violence, hatred, fear, and insecurity every day, and eventually he gets sick. . . . We need some guidelines, some preventive medicine, to protect ourselves, so we can become healthy again. We have to find a cure for our illness. We have to find something that is good, beautiful, and true in which we can take refuge.

When we drive a car, we are expected to observe certain rules so that we do not have an accident. Twenty-five hundred years ago, the Buddha offered certain guidelines to his lay students to help them live peaceful, wholesome, and happy lives. They were the Five Mindfulness Trainings, and at the foundation of each of these mindfulness trainings is mindfulness. With mindfulness, we are aware of what is going on in our bodies, our feelings, our minds, and the world, and we avoid doing harm to ourselves and others. Mindfulness protects us, our families, and our society, and ensures a safe and happy present and a safe and happy future. . . .

The Five Mindfulness Trainings are love itself. To love is to understand, protect, and bring well-being to the object of our love. The practice of the mindfulness trainings accomplishes this. We protect ourselves and we protect each other.

The translation of the Five Mindfulness Trainings presented in this book is new. It is the result of insights gained from practicing together as a community. A spiritual tradition is like a tree. It needs to be watered in order to bring forth new leaves and branches, so it can continue to be a living reality. We help the tree of Buddhism grow by living deeply the essence of reality, the practice of mindfulness trainings, concentration, and insight. If we continue to practice the mindfulness trainings deeply, in relation to our society and culture, I am confident that our children and their children will have an even better understanding of the Five Mindfulness Trainings and will obtain even deeper peace and joy. . . .

What is the best way to practice the mindfulness trainings? I do not know. I am still learning, along with you. I appreciate the phrase that is used in the Five Mindfulness Trainings: to "learn ways." We do not know everything. But we can minimize our ignorance. Confucius said, "To know that you don't know is the beginning of knowing." I think this is the way to practice. We should be modest and open so we can learn together. We need a Sangha, a community, to support us, and we need to stay in close touch with our society to practice the mindfulness trainings well. Many of today's problems did not exist at the time of the Buddha. Therefore, we have to look deeply together in order to develop the insights that will help us and our children find better ways to live wholesome, happy, and healthy lives.

When someone asks, "Do you care? Do you care about me? Do you care about life? Do you care about the Earth?", the best way to answer is to practice the Five Mindfulness Trainings. This is to teach with your actions and not just with words. If you really care, please practice these mindfulness trainings for your own protection and for the protection of other people and species. If we do our best to practice, a future will be possible for us, our children, and their children.

First Mindfulness Training

Aware of the suffering caused by the destruction of life, I am committed to cultivating compassion and learning ways to protect the lives of people, animals, plants, and minerals. I am determined not to kill, not to let others kill, and not to condone any act of killing in the world, in my thinking, and in my way of life.

Second Mindfulness Training

Aware of the suffering caused by exploitation, social injustice, stealing, and oppression, I am committed to cultivating loving-kindness and learning ways to work for the well-being of people, animals, plants, and minerals. I will practice generosity by sharing my time, energy, and material resources with those who are in real need. I am determined not to steal and not to possess anything that should belong to others. I will respect the property of others, but I will prevent others from profiting from human suffering or the suffering of other species on Earth.

Third Mindfulness Training

Aware of the suffering caused by sexual misconduct, I am committed to cultivating responsibility and learning ways to protect the safety and integrity of individuals, couples, families, and society. I am determined not to engage in sexual relations without love and a long-term commitment. To preserve the happiness of myself and others, I am determined to respect my commitments and the commitments of others. I will do everything in my power to protect children from sexual abuse and to prevent couples and families from being broken by sexual misconduct.

Fourth Mindfulness Training

Aware of the suffering caused by unmindful speech and the inability to listen to others, I am committed to cultivating loving speech and deep listening in order to bring joy and happiness to others and relieve others of their suffering. Knowing that words can create happiness or suffering, I am determined to speak truthfully, with words that inspire self-confidence, joy, and hope. I will not spread news that I do not know to be certain and will not criticize or condemn things of which I am not sure. I will refrain from uttering words that can cause division or discord, or that can cause the family or the community to break. I am determined to make all efforts to reconcile and resolve all conflicts, however small.

Fifth Mindfulness Training

Aware of the suffering caused by unmindful consumption, I am committed to cultivating good health, both physical and mental, for myself, my family, and my society by practicing mindful eating, drinking, and consuming. I will ingest only items that preserve peace, well-being, and joy in my body, in my consciousness, and in the collective body and consciousness of my family and society. I am determined not to use alcohol or any other intoxicant or to ingest foods or other items that contain toxins, such as certain programs, magazines, books, films, and conversations. I am aware that to damage my body or my consciousness with these poisons is to betray my ancestors, my parents, my society, and future generations. I will work to transform violence, fear, anger, and confusion in myself and in society by practicing a diet for myself and for society. I understand that a proper diet is crucial for self-transformation and for the transformation of society.

— For a Future To Be Possible

THE PATH OF TRANSFORMATION

During the time of the Buddha, the aim of the practice of many people was to be born and to live together with Brahma. It was similar to the Christian practice of wanting to go to Heaven to be with God. "In my Father's house there are many mansions," and you want to live in one of these mansions. For those who wanted to be with Brahma, the Buddha said, "Practice the four noble dwellings: love, compassion, joy, and impartiality." If we want to share one teaching of the Buddha with our Christian friends, it would be the same: "God is love, compassion, joy, and impartiality." If you want to be with God, practice these four dwellings. If you don't practice these four, no matter how much you pray or talk about being with God, going to Heaven will not be possible.

•

In Buddhism there are two kinds of practice — devotional and transformational. To practice devotion is to rely primarily on the power of another, who may be a buddha or a god. To practice transformation is to rely more on yourself and the path you are following. To be devoted to the Dharma is different from practicing the Dharma. When you say, "I take refuge in the Dharma," you may be showing your faith in it, but that is not the same as practicing the Dharma. To say "I want to become a doctor" is an expression of the determination to practice medicine. But to become a doctor, you have to spend seven or eight years studying and practicing medicine. When you say, "I take refuge in the Buddha, the Dharma, and the Sangha," this may be only the *willingness* to practice. It is not because you make this statement that you are already practicing. You enter the path of transformation when you begin to practice the things you pronounce. — *For a Future To Be Possible*

Many of us worry about the situation of the world. We don't know when the bombs will explode. We feel that we are on the edge of time. As individuals, we feel helpless, despairing. The situation is so dangerous, injustice is so widespread, the danger is so close. In this kind of situation, if we panic, things will only become worse. We need to remain calm, to see clearly. Meditation is to be aware, and to try to help.

I like to use the example of a small boat crossing the Gulf of Siam. In Vietnam there are many people, called boat people, who leave the country in small boats. Often the boats are caught in rough seas or storms, the people may panic, and boats can sink. But if even one person aboard can remain calm, lucid, knowing what to do and what not to do, he or she can help the boat survive. His or her expression — face, voice — communicates clarity and calmness, and people have trust in that person. They will listen to what he or she says. One such person can save the lives of many.

Our world is something like a small boat. Compared with the cosmos, our planet is a very small boat. We are about to panic because our situation is no better than the situation of the small boat in the sea. You know that we have more than fifty thousand nuclear weapons. Humankind has become a very dangerous species. We need people who can sit still and be able to smile, who can walk peacefully. We need people like that in order to save us. Mahayana Buddhism says that you are that person, that each of you is that person.   — *Being Peace*

INVITING THE BELL

May the sound of this bell penetrate deeply
into the cosmos.
In even the darkest spots, may living beings
hear it clearly
so their suffering will cease,
understanding arise in their hearts,
and they can transcend the path of anxiety
and sorrow.

— Stepping into Freedom

MODERN SPIRITUAL MASTERS SERIES

Dietrich Bonhoeffer

*Writings Selected with an Introduction
by Robert Coles*

ISBN 1-57075-194-3.

Henri Nouwen

*Writings Selected with an Introduction
by Robert A. Jonas*

ISBN 1-57075-197-8.

Anthony de Mello

*Writings Selected with an Introduction
by William Dych, S.J.*

ISBN 1-57075-283-4.

Thomas Merton

*Essential Writings
Selected with an Introduction
by Christine Bochen*

ISBN 1-57075-331-8.

Pierre Teilhard de Chardin

*Writings Selected with an Introduction
by Ursula King*

ISBN 1-57075-248-6.